MW00808207

Once AND Future CHRIST

WHERE EAST MEETS WEST

Nayaswami Hriman McGilloway

CRYSTAL CLARITY PUBLISHERS Commerce, California

CRYSTAL CLARITY PUBLISHERS
1123 Goodrich Blvd | Commerce, California
crystalclarity.com | clarity@crystalclarity.com
800.424.1055

ISBN   978-1-56589-118-0 (print)
ISBN   978-1-56589-594-2 (e-book)
Library of Congress Cataloging-in-Publication Data:
   LCCN 2023003114 (print) | LCCN 2023003115 (e-book)

Cover design by Tejindra Scott Tully
Interior design and layout by Michele Madhavi Molloy

The *Joy Is Within You* symbol is registered by Ananda
Church of Self-Realization of Nevada County, California.

Contents

Preface

The Need and the Source

WE LIVE IN AN AGE WHERE THE NEED FOR A FRESH understanding of God's presence in our lives is great because the darkness of ignorance, too, is great. The potential to destroy ourselves and planet earth is all too present.

Adding to our predicament is the simple fact that religion — which ought to unite us in peace and harmony — tends to divide us. Why should the fact that great spiritual teachers and saints have lived in all lands and in all times be a source of conflict? It is not as though they disagree among themselves on whether we should strive to love God and to express that love to all.

Yet neither do we need a "one world" religion. The different religions reflect the variations in cultures and history and differing points of view of the single "elephant" of truth.* The diversity that exists in the various faiths, prayers and rituals are precious and sacred.

---

* Surely the reader knows the famous story of the blind men and the elephant: each one touching a different part of the elephant insists that the elephant is as he experienced it.

What is needed is a new understanding of what the various faith traditions point to: the potential for the elevation of our human nature into our divine nature, into the image of our Creator.

What, then, divides people of faith from a new understanding? The first is the prejudice that orthodox believers of each religion have against other religions. The second is the disillusionment and skepticism of non-religionists who are put off by religious bigotry. It doesn't help that this latter group gleefully contrasts the usefulness of science with the unprovable assertions of religious dogma. That dogmatists and skeptics alike might find renewed inspiration and acceptance would be an incalculable benefit to humanity. Truly the result would be, to quote the Book of Revelations, "the healing of the nations."*

Paramhansa Yogananda is known throughout the world as the author of what has become a twentieth century classic of spiritual literature, *Autobiography of a Yogi.*† Yogananda was born in 1893 in India and came to America in 1920. He traveled through the United States attracting thousands to his lectures and classes, becoming one of the nation's most sought-after inspirational speakers of the 1930's. In 1925 he established the headquarters for his work in Los Angeles.

Yogananda was sent to the West to show that the same, unchanging divine message illuminates all true faiths. He gave special emphasis to the teachings of Jesus Christ (New Testament) and the teachings of Lord Krishna (Bhagavad Gita). His is not a syncretic concoction nor a dilution of their respective teachings into a tasteless alphabet soup of "-isms." It was

* Revelations 22:2
† The original 1946 edition of *Autobiography of a Yogi* is published by Crystal Clarity Publishers.

his intent, and the intention of those who sent him, to reveal the underlying unity and universal applicability of both Jesus' message and that of Krishna. This book is inspired to both explain and to explore the details and implications of his insights into the teachings of these two illumined world teachers. I believe millions of Christians know intuitively that Jesus' life and teachings are for everyone but, burdened by the exclusive claims of Christian dogma, too many Christians and Christian leaders feel they must view as second-class anyone who does not believe as they do.

Paramhansa Yogananda stated that "Jesus was crucified once but his teachings have been crucified daily ever since." Yogananda coined the term "Churchianity" to distinguish the true teachings of Jesus Christ from the institutional teachings of the churches. His intention was not so much to criticize but to elevate and inspire. No organization holds a monopoly on truth and among sincere seekers is not truth crucified daily by human attachments and general ignorance? As Pontius Pilate asked Jesus: "What is truth?"* As we see in the investigations of science, finding the truth behind the appearance of matter and energy is no simple or easy task.

Scholars and historians who have studied the history of Christianity testify to its ever-evolving forms, challenges, successes, and betrayals. And yet, it has survived, I believe, by the spiritual power of its underlying truth. Whatever one might say about Christians, churches, or Christianity, the life of Jesus Christ changed the course of history; it has produced great saints, great art, music, literature, and has inspired true seekers down through the ages. We acknowledge that abuses and grave errors

* John 18:38

have also occurred. Yogananda pointed out that the "true custodians of religion" are the saints, not the prelates and theologians. It is the saints who live, and not merely speak, the "truth that shall make us free."*

This book is based on the insights, commentaries, and intuitive realization of Paramhansa Yogananda who was one of the twentieth century's spiritual giants.

In the Hindu "Bible," the Bhagavad Gita, it is taught that in every age God responds to the silent prayers of human hearts and sends to earth God-realized souls to bring afresh the eternal message of our soul's immortality.

In this book, I hope to share insights inspired by Yogananda's original writings and by the writings of one of Yogananda's most prolific and publicly active direct disciples: Swami Kriyananda, founder of the worldwide work called "Ananda."

One of the most precious gifts that Yogananda brought to modern culture is meditation and the advanced technique of meditation that is called Kriya Yoga. But meditation and Kriya Yoga are not the focus of this book.

It would be a fair question to ask, "For whom has this book been written?" It is my sincere hope that Christians who seek in their hearts to expand beyond the exclusive claims of Christian dogma will find hope, inspiration, and wisdom for their courageous journey. And that those who love India's timeless wisdom will enjoy seeing that wisdom shining through the words of Jesus Christ and the prophets.

An explanation here may be helpful. Paramhansa Yogananda did not approach the Bible in the manner of

---

* John 8:32

scholars. He did not examine the original meanings of Greek or Aramaic words, or their evolution; nor did he speculate on the errors or interpretations of translators; nor did he imagine conniving plots by theologians, or church administrators down through the centuries. Yogananda isn't attacking anything or anyone. He is using the ancient wisdom of India to pierce the veil of Christian dogma to show their similarity. Having taken up residence and citizenship in America in the twentieth century, Yogananda brings a contemporary perspective and language to this task. Yogananda's teachings are rooted in a worldview and spiritual tradition that reaches far back into the history of India's greatest saints and sages. One need not be a follower of Yogananda to appreciate these insights. But I hope that those who are attuned to Yogananda will appreciate my attempt to share those insights.

Introduction

My Search

I COMPLETED SIXTEEN YEARS OF CATHOLIC EDUCATION — from first grade (1956) through university (1972). I even attended a preparatory high school seminary thinking I might become a priest. In grammar school I learned that the word catholic meant universal. I was thrilled, even at a young age, to hear this. For indeed, the search for universality has characterized my spiritual journey even though it took me far from the faith of my childhood. Or has it?

Albert Einstein, one of the greatest scientists who ever lived, was driven by the conviction that underlying the diversity and complexity of nature must surely exist a unifying principle. Religion strives to answer the great questions of life: the how and why of creation; the existence and nature of the Creator; the purpose of human life; and the paradox that a loving Creator tolerates suffering and evil.

What I didn't know then, and appreciate more fully now, was that reason and intellect could only *describe* the taste of a mango but could not give the *experience* of the mango's intoxicating flavor. I am reminded of a charming story about the mother of Krishna as a toddler: she could not find a string long enough to tie him up (so she could do her chores) because who can tie up Infinity? Philosophy and theology are like the menu for a restaurant: the menu can't satisfy your appetite.

One of the most significant trends in human consciousness in our times is the awareness that an intellectual grasp or definition of reality is NOT a substitute for the *experience* of reality. Applied to spiritual teachings, this trend is related to the success and popular acceptance of science along with the growing rejection of untested beliefs or unprovable dogmas. It is reflected in the popularity of yoga and meditation, the growth of the "spiritual but not religious" movement, and a decline in affiliation with religious faiths.

I came of age in the San Francisco Bay Area at a time of great social and cultural ferment. At the University of Santa Clara, a Jesuit college, comparative religious studies were popular and speakers like Alan Watts were in high demand. "Up the street" in San Francisco, the Haight Ashbury district was in full bloom and across the Bay in Oakland tear gas and rocks exploded in protest of what was happening in a faraway country in Southeast Asia.

I look back at the textbooks I studied on Buddhism and Hinduism and realize that while their scholarly analyses missed the mark of the heart-that-knows, it was enough to start me on the path of meditation. I screened off the back part of my garage to create a place to study and meditate. Next to my "cave" was an old wringer washing machine which, as I look back, was a symbol for my own turbulence and confusion (and probably my meditations, as well). So far as I knew at the time, there were no classes on meditation and there was certainly no internet in 1970. Fortunately, I remained undeterred.

After working a few years after college, I left my job and sold what little I had and went off to Europe with my best friend from college. We both were meditators. We thought we were just going to drive around Europe for the summer. Meeting other young travelers, however, we learned that one could drive all the way to India. To us Europe seemed rather tame and familiar, so, drawn by the light of Asia, we began our overland journey as soon as we could.*

This isn't a story of that amazing journey, but amid a host of adventures we drove down one side of India, into Sri Lanka, and back up the other side into Nepal. For me, the point of that trip relevant to this book is that I didn't find what I was looking for. The truth was, as I look back, that I simply wasn't ready to commit my life to the spiritual path.

On our return journey to Europe, we sold the VW van in Kabul, Afghanistan. From Kabul, we flew back to Delhi and then from there to London, Seattle, and finally San Francisco. Somewhere over Tehran in a darkened and nearly empty plane, I had the "aha moment" that marked a turning point in my life. It was mostly a wordless "Aha" but over the decades I've filled in the blanks with words as my own understanding clarified. I intuitively saw that I had been holding the spiritual life at bay because I was unwilling to surrender my will to the divine will. While at the time I defined that

---

* To drive east we needed an insurance document called a "Carnet de Passages" for our car. While waiting in Greece, we obtained it from the Auto Club in Germany where we had purchased the car.

independence as a disdain for organized religion, I gradually began to understand my hesitation in terms of the ego's surrender to God. (A work in progress, mind you.)

Upon arriving in Monterey, California, the home of my parents, where I sought temporary employment, I was soon to meet my future wife, Padma. It was she who handed me a copy of *Autobiography of a Yogi* by Paramhansa Yogananda. I stayed up all night reading, laughing, and crying. I never looked back and never felt the need to question or examine my intuitive realization that the teachings of Self-realization as Yogananda shared them was for me.

From Padma I learned about the Ananda Community northeast of Sacramento, California and it wasn't long before we moved to nearby Nevada City.

It was here that I met Swami Kriyananda, a direct disciple of Paramhansa Yogananda. "Swamiji" spoke and wrote with a clarity one does not find among mere scholars. The rhythm of his words and their succinct, scripture-like potency echoed that of Yogananda's. Kriyananda's grasp of how to bridge Western thinking, culture, and challenges to the ancient teachings of India was not only a mark of his refined intellect but was embedded in his personal realization.

The answer to my prayer for universality was answered in such large "gobs" that it has taken decades of meditation, teaching, reading, and discussion to get to a place where I felt ready to share these inspirations. And so, let's begin our adventure together.

The Nature of Spiritual Truths

I T MAY BE USEFUL TO CONSIDER A DISTINCTION THAT ordinarily we find no need for: metaphysical truths as distinct from religion. Metaphysical teachings include the how and why of creation, the existence and nature of God, virtue, evil, suffering, salvation, subtler realms of existence, after-death states, and higher beings. These subjects are not primarily material in nature for they are thus "meta-physical."

In a culture as materialistic as our own, religion tends to be focused on rituals and ethical behavior. While religion naturally offers metaphysical teachings on topics such as heaven, hell, and salvation, those tend to be of secondary importance. It is enough to simply believe and accept, let us say, Jesus Christ as one's personal savior. Otherwise, the concern and interest of most churches tends to be that of attending services and supporting one's church, obeying ethical standards, and supporting humanitarian goals, justice, and human rights. I'll be the first to admit that humanity at large is not entirely unjustified in focusing on present, material realities. In addition, humanity at large is not yet sufficiently refined in consciousness to appreciate subtler realities. In this department, science is far ahead of the rest of humanity — peering into the origins of life with tools far superior to our senses and even our power of reason.

Concepts of quantum entanglement and string theory defy common sensory experience, yet they are largely accepted by their votaries and therefore, by extension, you and me, "lay disciples" of the religion of science. I am not saying that metaphysical truths should affront our common sense but who can truly say that the miracles of Jesus Christ are that farfetched simply because we haven't personally experienced them? We use computers and cell phones everyday but our familiarity with them doesn't require that we understand how they work.

Scripture, when it deals with metaphysical truths like grace, healing, and after-death states of consciousness, claims for its source the experience of transcendent reality. Just because our conscious mind and memory cannot validate such statements does not automatically render them false. As we accept the testimony of quantum physicists or astrophysicists based on their intelligence and veracity, why would we not be open to the testimony of one whose life has changed world history: Jesus Christ, and even, by extension, his direct disciples who were willing to die in defense of their testimony? The validity of metaphysical truths may be as inferential as that of quantum physics. The proof of spiritual living is found in the answer to the question: "Does it work?" Are people happier, wiser, healthier, more forgiving and selfless? Modern studies are indeed showing the efficacy of the inner spiritual life and outward, spiritual fellowship.

There is another aspect to the transcendental nature of metaphysical realities: self-mastery. I have heard it said that after Albert Einstein's Theory of Relativity was published there were perhaps as few as ten people who could understand it. There may be many more now in the twenty-first century, but let's face it, those who understand $E=mc^2$ comprise an insignificant percentage of the seven or eight billion people on this planet.

How many people can speak knowledgeably about quantum physics, string theory, quantum entanglement, or black holes? Add to this the "multi-verse" as opposed to the universe. How many brain surgeons are there in the human population?

So why might there not be in the metaphysical realms, "masters" who have achieved transcendent states of consciousness? Jesus Christ, for those who count themselves as his disciples, was certainly one such master. The fact that I'm not an astronaut doesn't preclude the human potential to be one. Anything one human can do, others can and have done also.

Consider also that metaphysical truths relate to a unitive reality rather than a dualistic one.* I find it simpler and more practical to call this the "Both-And" view of reality rather than the logic-burdened "Either-Or" version. My life has been enriched by using Both-And as a handle by which to resolve conflicts and differing points of view. One of the great controversies about Jesus Christ is illustrated in his question to his disciples: "Who do men say I AM?" The question was not necessarily resolved by Peter's now famous reply: "Thou art the living Christ." For centuries thereafter, intense debate and even violence has attended the conflicting responses to this question. Reason may want us to say that Jesus was "*either*" human "*or*" divine, but a higher reality may suggest Jesus was *both* human *and* divine. If so, are we also that?

Because words reflect intellectual concepts, words are only symbols used to describe experience. Words point to, but do not replace, the experience itself. Language is by its very

---

* God, ONE and indivisible, is unitive; creation, by contrast, reflects the pairs of opposites, always in flux.

nature Either-Or, not Both-And. We find this illustrated dramatically in the rising controversy that rejects gender identification. Many languages require a binary tag to be applied to all sorts of neutral nouns like apples, rivers, and mountains. Language is inherently Either-Or, while stories, parables, and poetry which play an important role in scriptures can paint a picture of non-dual realities, that is, Both-And.

Not surprisingly therefore, we find metaphysical teachings couched in story-pictures which, like music, can touch a deeper level of our awareness than the intellect. Pictures are truer to life's experience than words.

To return to my own journey, this book is based on the wisdom-teachings of Paramhansa Yogananda on the Bible, with special emphasis on the New Testament. Throughout this book I will use terms such as *Sanatan Dharma* or the Vedas or the Bhagavad Gita to indicate the great tradition and teachings of India. Some specific references will accompany these terms but usually I make only a general statement.[*]

In addition, I draw upon the writings of Swami Kriyananda who, being trained and commissioned by Yogananda, wrote extensively on these very same subjects.[†] Whatever I have added here and there I hope will be easy to distinguish.

[*] *Sanatan Dharma* is the indigenous name for what evolved into Hinduism, but I am specifically using it to refer to the core values and teachings rather than the customs and rituals we associate with Hinduism. The "Vedas" refer to a large body of scripture which is extremely diverse and which, for my purposes, includes the Upanishads. But this book is not a scholarly presentation of India's teachings, so my references are general and usually casual. The Bhagavad Gita is said to be the distillation of *Sanatan Dharma*, including the historically earlier Vedas and Upanishads. In quoting the Bhagavad Gita, however, I do sometimes provide specific references because Yogananda himself wrote a commentary on this sacred text.

[†] A partial list of Swami Kriyananda's writings on this subject include book titles such as *Promise of Immortality, Revelations of Christ, Rays of the One Light*, and *The Beatitudes*, published by Crystal Clarity Publishers.

Once and Future
CHRIST

PART ONE

East Meets West

Chapter 1

In the Beginning

Is God Watching from Above, or....?

WHEN I CONSIDER THE IMMENSE COMPLEXITY OF creation and of the human body, I marvel when I come across simplistic descriptions of God described as sitting on a throne being worshiped by throngs of angels and saints, or contrastingly, indwelling in every atom of creation. I ask the reader to indulge my "Both-And" mantra. It is my "happy place." I go there when being chased by that monster of reality called Paradox. So, I am hoping we can take this journey together without having to imagine we can define Infinity.

One of the ironies of the Book of Genesis in the Old Testament is the lack of interest in how the world or human beings were created. There's no explanation offered for how exactly God stepped into human history and human lives. I say "ironic" because our own society is so heaven-bent on figuring out how everything works. It seems the ancients either lacked curiosity, already knew the answer to that question, or had a very different interest in life than we do.

It is important at this juncture to step back from our culture and appreciate how focused we are on "how things work." Swami Kriyananda, in his own life story, *The New Path*, explains that he and his father did not share the same approach to life because his father, a geologist for Esso, was interested in *how* things worked while his son, young Donald Walters, was interested in *why.** As I say often to students, the real religion of our culture is science. If science says it is so, then it must be so.† In former times, if a prophet said, "it is so," then it was deemed to be so.

The Book of Genesis simply says that God made the world in six days and humanity from the dust of the earth. Well, okay, but how? Could it be that the ancients were already so conscious of God's presence that the question of "how" was of no interest? Was the "how" self-evident to them?

God: Personal or Cosmic?

In the Old Testament we read of God walking with Adam and Eve in the Garden of Eden. God speaks to Noah, Jacob, and others. Before destroying the towns of Sodom and Gomorrah, God visits Jacob and Sarah and goes for a walk into town. The God of the Old Testament seems like just another person. I think that is a wonderful way to relate to God, but is this what God IS?

Some Christians calculate the era of Adam and Eve in the Garden of Eden somewhere around 4,000 B.C. Thousands of years later, the Upanishads of India, Plato and St. John the Apostle described God in more abstract and impersonal

* Swami Kriyananda, *The New Path*, Crystal Clarity Publishers.
† In the recent years of the COVID-19 pandemic and in the case of Global Warming, we see a distinct erosion in acceptance of the testimony of science among humanity.

terms. Keeping in mind the mantra "Both-And," logic itself suggests that God, being Infinite "by nature," can therefore be both impersonal and personal; both Infinite and infinitesimal; both "other" and omnipresent.

Did God Create the Universe or Did God Become the Universe?

Are we ready to fearlessly ask the question the ancients failed to ask? "How did God create the universe?" We could put the question a different way: "How does something come from nothing?" It just so happens that science is asking this same question: "What preceded the Big Bang?" For now, let's stick with Genesis because the testimony of Genesis is the genesis of a fundamental difference between East and West. Ultimately, we will show that this seeming difference is an illusion, but we must first examine in detail this difference.

What is this fundamental difference? Orthodox Christian teachings depict God and Jesus Christ as separate from you and me. By contrast, the teachings of India posit that divinity resides *within* the creation. Just as the orthodox Jews of Jesus' time were shocked that Jesus would claim to be the son of God, so orthodox Christians are repelled by the Indian view that God resides everywhere and in everyone. Christians could accept that the "Word was made flesh" in the person of Jesus Christ, but it seems they are reluctant to let the idea spread any further.

Separation from God

The separation of man from God depicted in the fall of Adam and Eve in Genesis demands in the fitness of things a reconciliation between God and man. The impulse in humans to bring the big picture into a unitive focus demands it. From the Eastern point of view, in becoming the universe (including human beings) God continues to reside within us. From this view, it would seem that no separation has occurred. So, which is it?

The difference, while ultimately insubstantial, is the basis for the two approaches to God which, while seemingly "Either-Or," we will discover are, in fact, "Both-And." I am teasing the reader to a certain degree, but I am serious as well. Let me say in simple terms that "separation" requires "reconciliation" while "indwelling" requires "re-awakening." The one emphasizes repentance, the other, self-expansion.

So, How Did God Do the Deed?

If one assumes there were no natural elements floating around in empty space that could be conscripted to start a universe and be "pressed" into a black hole so the whole thing could start off with a "big bang," then it would be rational to conclude that God somehow made the material universe out of the "stuff" of Self, which is to say out of No-thing (material). While the Book of Genesis doesn't say *how* it happened, in India it is taught that God created the universe by *becoming* the universe.

I can see why Genesis kept the creation story on an anthropomorphic level: God, viewed as a person, creates "things," including humankind, just like we do. And if the author's purpose is to tell the story of humanity, it's easier to get there sooner rather than later.

If the story said that God *became* the universe it creates a great many questions which only a more abstractly inquisitive person would find interesting. Questions such as:

1. If God became the universe, then God became me?
2. Am I God?
3. Is that rock over there also God?
4. Is evil and suffering God, too?

Can you see why the author of Genesis was more interested in getting to the important story of humankind?

The Great Illusion: Duality

Using our imagination to think of God before creation took place, we could presumably conclude that God has no body, no name, no form, no attributes in the ordinary psychological sense. The common assumption is to view God as whole and complete, lacking nothing emotionally or knowledge-wise. In India in ancient texts, God is described as *Satchidanandam*: ever-existing (immortal), ever-conscious (Self-aware, omniscient and omnipresent), ever-new bliss.* God needed no-thing and no-body. It wouldn't be a big leap to imagine, further, that God was perfectly still. How can there be movement without space and objects?

The initial idea to create the universe must have been a bit like dropping a rock into a perfectly still pond: God's "big idea" must have produced an enormous energy wave going "out" from God's perfect tranquility. At the center God remained unruffled. In so Being and Doing, God at the center remained God the Father of Creation, which is to say, God beyond creation and untouched by its fluctuations.

---

* Why the "bliss" part? If God is everything, then God is whole and complete. If conscious existence is whole, how could it not be happy? Bliss is that form of "happy'" that is not conditioned by temporary circumstances. It has to be "ever-new" lest it be boring or lest, in the absence of its opposite, it cannot exist at all. Ok, so it's a paradox.

But the shock wave of energy is also God. As a word re-flects a thought, so the "Word" of God was the "beginning" of creation: and the "Word" was "with God," and the "Word was God," "and without him was not anything made that was made."*

Those rippling waves are the energized and manifested "Word" of God's thought and intention. A wave, by definition, must have a trough. All creation oscillates from the quantum level to the vast universe. All things in creation are polar: positive or negative.

Quantum physics reveals that even the most substantial object consists mostly of space and energy and that the ap-pearance of an object is essentially an illusion made in part by the object's electromagnetism and only in reference to other objects with an electromagnetic field like its own.

But while those great waves of creation have their visible (measurable and energetic) manifestation, they also contain within the invisible element of the guiding consciousness and intelligence that generated them. Why? Because they are naught but a vibration or wave extending from the con-sciousness of God. How could consciousness, then, be absent from the wave?

This bifurcation of God between thought and energy in the *becoming* of creation is the duality of spirit and matter. The human body, for example, reveals my form but my thoughts are invisible. Every act I perform is visible but my intention, though sometimes revealed by the nature of the action, is also potentially unknown or at least not obvious. I can do a good deed because I am inspired, or I can do it for approval from others. The deed itself does not necessarily reveal the intention.

* John 1:1

Thus, the creation in its visible form hints of a Creator, but at the same time masks the Creator's invisible spirit or consciousness. To achieve the illusion of an infinity of separate objects, an unceasing oscillating motion is required; a pendulum of opposites was necessary.

Science tells us that space is not empty and that out of the seemingly empty space pops the quanta that give rise to electromagnetic fields and the appearance of quantum particles. Is the scientific perception of space the equivalent of the invisible consciousness out of which comes the appearance of objects?*

Therefore, *Sanatan Dharma* says that God became the universe by separating consciousness from form; male from female; light from dark; heat from cold; and so on.

---

* At present it has been estimated that the visible universe amounts to only five percent of the total calculated universe consisting of matter and energy. The rest is "dark," meaning invisible and consisting of "dark matter" and "dark energy."

Chapter 2

Creation, Creativity, and Science

HOW COULD THE MIND OF GOD CREATE THIS AMAZING and infinitely complex universe? Let's explore a few scenarios taken from human experience.

Power of Thought

Consider this: You suddenly have the inspiration to write the "great American novel." Excited and inspired, ideas for the plot begin to flow into your mind. You sit to write and before long you discover what other authors before you have learned: the personalities, motives, and actions of the characters unfold as if on their own. You are simply the scribe.

Now, imagine this scenario: You are God, but you're all alone. Sure, you're infinitely awesome and infinitely powerful.* You can do and have anything but there isn't any-thing around you. Are you just going to sit there and BE? That's no fun. Sure, you're in bliss, but is that enough? It's not that you *must* play because, after all, you are already bubbling with

* But wait: how does being powerful fit into having no form; no space; no objects; only consciousness? Easy: in our minds we can do anything, right?

joy, but then you think to your Self, "What's joy if there is nothing to do and no one to share it with?"*

But then you think, "Hmm, how is a no-thing Me going to create some-thing?

You've heard the expression "If we build it, they will come." God says, "If I think it, it exists." Like that great American novel, that's where ideas come from: no-where. Ideas come from no-thing; they are born of consciousness. (Isn't God often defined as Pure Consciousness?)

Put poetically, "Out of the silence of consciousness, came the song of creation."†

How else could God have created the great drama of the universe except by the power of thought? Assuming God didn't speak a language like English, I imagine that the thought was more like a powerful projection of an image or a grand visualization.

Before moving on to the stages of creation in which objects appear both real and yet separate, and some objects (like you and me) have initiative, desires, free will, creativity, and the ability to be good or bad, let us finish a few thoughts on the power of thoughts.

It's All in Your Head

Writing a novel is not much different than dreaming. It's all in your head, that is. If you were as awesomely bright as God, your "thought" of creating a universe, proceeding as it does only from your own consciousness, is essentially no different than a dream. Assuming God doesn't have a

---

* Spoiler alert: no explanation of why the universe was created can ever satisfy the heart.

† A phrase taken from a song by Swami Kriyananda titled "Thunder of AUM!" It is sung each Sunday at the Festival of Light ceremony at Ananda temples.

subconscious, let us assume that God's "dream" is a bit more conscious than our nocturnal ones. But for all that it's still in the Godhead.

There is no-thing but God-consciousness out of which creation can be manifested. Unless we posit that God doesn't exist, we are basically stuck with this truth by force of sheer logic. So, let's keep going.

It's Not Easy: It Takes ENERGY

It's not easy to write the great American novel. It takes a lot of discipline, hard work, faith, courage, and the creative nectar of the Muses. All those things put together we'll call *energy*: intelligent, purposeful, and creative. If there's one thing that modern science tells us exists in abundance in our universe, it's *energy*. In the mind of science, energy seems to be an unconscious force, but then to misquote Forrest Gump, "Consciousness is as consciousness does."

Let us consider two rather curious aspects of the experience of having ideas. (Not ordinary humdrum ideas, but "big" ideas like the great American novel or creating an entire universe.)

First: we can legitimately say "I had an idea" but it would be far more accurate to say, "An idea came to me." The novelist "tunes" the dial of the mind to the story and out of nowhere come characters and the plot. Our intention and effort are needed but it's not muscular effort nor is it even "merely" rational. We don't know where these ideas come from, though if we, by practice, have gotten good at our skill we find appropriate ideas just come. We naturally take a certain amount of credit for them. Usually, they come because we need them or invite them, but sometimes important ideas just appear. Nonetheless, ideas come in relation to who we are. Einstein didn't receive symphonies, nor did Beethoven receive solutions to mathematical problems.

Second: when an idea comes, we have a response to it. This is the second curious aspect: that an idea, coming from nowhere, sparks in us an outpouring of energy! I'm going to abandon the analogy to our personal experience because our reaction to an idea may be traced to subconscious latencies. But God, in responding to the idea of creation, is presumably free of subconscious impulses. Either way, the energy to manifest an idea seems to come bundled with the idea itself: both from the same "no-where." Thought and energy, in other words, are a bit like matter and energy: two sides of the same coin. I admit science may endorse the latter and not (yet) the former, but the possibility seems worthy of consideration. In my personal experience of having an idea come to me, the time lapse between the idea and my response to it seems all but nonexistent.

Thought and Energy: Two Sides of the Coin of Matter?

Since science tells us that there's a whole lot of energy out there in our universe, the possibility that I raise suggests there's an *idea* "inside of" it. Or just "behind" it! Is it possible that not only do ideas come from nowhere but those ideas somehow, secretly, or invisibly, come pre-bundled with the potential energy to manifest them? While science cannot yet go this far with us, we can absolutely corroborate the fact that ideas can sometimes release so much energy in us that our lives are changed (and maybe the lives of others, too).

Since we are on the subject of big ideas and the big energy they can generate, what about those humans whose big
ideas have changed world history? For the purposes of my
subject, I naturally look to the life of Jesus Christ. Like it
or not, we cannot deny that in only three years Jesus Christ
changed the course of history. His personal relationship with
a few disciples released through them an enormous output
of energy which rippled forward through the lives of thousands and onward to include millions of believers. The history of Christianity is necessarily an all-too human one, for
it includes in its drama the lives of saints and sinners alike.
Should we be at all surprised that the descent into human
form of even a tiny "piece" of the power that created this
universe be the spiritual equivalent of an atomic bomb?

What Am I Missing?

As the splitting of an atom releases enormous energy
according to $E=mc^2$, perhaps we might imagine that intention and intelligence, however subtle, contain the energy
necessary to bring into manifestation the visible forms of
the creation.* All we can say at this point in history is that
it seems like this may be the case. This conclusion, while
not (yet) provable, seems to me like the conclusion that
God must have "become" the universe because there was
no-thing other than Consciousness with which to make it.
While to me this seems self-evident, I confess that neither
Yogananda nor Swami Kriyananda put it this way.

---

* After his death, Albert Einstein's brain was preserved. Its physical size was not
notably larger than others but the instinct to want to know the source of that much
intelligence was natural enough. As energy is subtler and more powerful than matter (because matter is frozen energy), so mind-stuff, though invisible and all but
motionless, is potential energy and, at its source is more powerful. Science is either
not likely to prove this or is at least a long way from it at this time.

Science and Metaphysics Share a Question

Scientists are beginning to speculate that there's an enormous amount of energy "out there." As we metaphysicians might be puzzled over how God's big idea became a very big universe, so scientists seem to have a similar problem in their own realm. Their calculations indicate that they are missing an enormous amount of both energy and matter. Not knowing what to do, scientists have concluded that the missing matter needs a name and so they've called it dark matter. Turns out they are also missing a whole lot of energy. So, yup, they call the missing energy dark energy. As Einstein revealed to us, matter and energy are two sides of the same coin.

If our beloved scientists are missing an enormous amount of energy, maybe we metaphysicians, theologians, or God-seeking devotees might just admit that both we and Genesis have yet to find the "missing link" between God Consciousness and matter. Perhaps that's not a coincidence.*

To put a fine point on the potential connection being highlighted here, scientists go on to say that according to their calculations the known visible universe of mass-energy constitutes only five to six percent of the total, the rest being dark energy and dark matter.† Thus, I say to you, the reader, that if scientists can speculate so broadly about something so big but unknown, maybe metaphysical teachings about gods, goddesses, angels, demons, spirits, the causal universe, the astral universe, life force, and souls are worthy of our consideration. Just as the calculations and instruments necessary

* Someone once defined a coincidence as "God preferring to remain anonymous."
† Scientists have postulated that dark energy constitutes about sixty-eight percent and dark matter twenty-seven percent. A science denier recently announced the discovery of "*Doesn't Matter*" (ha, ha).

to detect dark energy and matter are of the utmost sophistication, why wouldn't we accept that it takes a higher level of
refined consciousness to pierce the veil of matter to see the
living etheric world of higher beings?*

"What About Me?"

Let's pick up these invisible realities from a more personal point of view. Contemplate for a moment how much
of what is "you" takes place invisibly between your head
and your heart. Most of what is "you" and "me" (as we
imagine ourselves to be) is in thought, memory, imagination, and emotions: all one-hundred percent invisible and
largely undetectable except as broadly differentiated brain
waves. Even a worldly person who is only concerned about
their outward appearance, social and economic status, and
sense enjoyments is still living primarily in their mind.

We cannot escape the importance of the non-visible
realities that stand as the source of the outer forms we
call "me." Saints and yogis are famous in worldly circles for
demonstrating "mind over matter." From Jesus Christ to
Buddha, Krishna to St. Francis, overcoming pain and even
death is the characteristic most noted by ordinary people
when they speak about such great beings. The relatively
new field of near-death studies is accumulating evidence
that consciousness is independent of the brain. As someone
once joked, "the brain doesn't matter."

* String theorists speculate that matter comes into being via tiny vibrating strings.
Are these strings, which cannot be proven by experiments, the missing link of the
subtle energy-vibration of thought that manifests an idea into an object?

A Universe of Vibration

Both metaphysical teachings and science seem to converge in their emphasis on rates of vibration as the explanation for why objects appear separate from one another. What do we mean by vibration?

Let's conduct a thought-experiment (like Einstein did): I am conscious and self-aware but not otherwise engaged in thoughts (maybe I'm looking out the window at a panorama). Then a thought appears in my mind. At that point the thought, relative to the peaceful state of awareness that preceded it, is like a small pebble thrown into a serene pond. The thought, you see, is a vibration, very subtle movement. A vibration (like the rock that was tossed) has energy. Thus, thought is a tiny burst of energy, albeit extremely subtle. As thoughts in our minds often tumble one after the other, thoughts, like the wavelets generated by the rock hitting the pond, generate not just more thoughts but also more energy. While we can easily distinguish a thought from the energy needed to put the thought into motion, we cannot deny that the thought itself is a form of energy. Nonetheless, the energetic quantum of thought is so subtle that perhaps we'll call it: elemental *vibration*.

Science and Vedanta agree that the seeming separateness of two objects is, in short, an illusion. I don't melt into the chair I'm sitting on because the electromagnetic vibrations of the atoms and molecules (and other energy particles) of each item are sufficiently different in their rates of vibration. The proportion of space to particles in my body and in my chair is overwhelmingly in favor of empty space.* It

* So that's what mystics mean when they declare before God: "I am nothing!"

is, perhaps, the same no-thing and no-where from which thoughts emerge. God, said to be consciousness itself, is purported to be omnipresent in all creation. So also, is space. Another coincidence?

If our material universe is dominated by invisible energy and matter, and if our personal reality is similarly dominated by thoughts, emotions, and energy, why would we be surprised at the great feats of power and energy attributed to those whose minds dominate matter?

Chapter 3

The Trinity

Is God Wholly Separate from Us?

NOW YOU MIGHT OBJECT TO THE IDEA THAT GOD became the universe because you harken back to God walking in the Garden of Eden with Adam and Eve. In that view of God, God seems separate from us. Indeed, in our *own* view of God in daily life, God is all too obviously "missing in action." But don't forget our mantra: "Both-And".

Because while much of the Bible describes God as "other," the saints and even theologians speak of God as triune: God the Father, beyond creation (untouched by the creation); God the Son, born into human form; and God the Holy Ghost, the Spirit that reveals all truth. Other Christian teachings hold that in the Eucharist ritual of the Mass, bread and wine are transmuted into the body and blood of Jesus Christ; or the teaching that the body of believers (Christians) constitute the body of Christ in the world.

Christian mystics speak of having visions of Jesus and some, including Old Testament prophets, speak of God appearing in impersonal forms such as light or sound (as a voice). Saints and theologians speak of God as omnipresent (in creation); God hears our prayers: "Your Father knows what things you have need of before you ask him."* And Jesus Christ said, "before Abraham was, I AM," and is described as He through whom the "world was made."†

God IN Creation is Unavoidable

The immanence of God in creation triggers other questions and paradoxes, most notably the existence of evil and suffering. Every world teacher has confronted this paradox. Few Christians realize that in India the concept of the Trinity also exists. Notwithstanding the questions that result, this teaching is unavoidable and necessarily true when one contemplates the process of creating some-thing from no-thing.

Is the Trinity Pantheism?

The famous Christian apologist C.S. Lewis has distinguished India's teachings from Christianity describing Hinduism with the loaded word "pantheism." He admitted his relative lack of knowledge of Eastern teachings, and it seems that he assumes that in India every rock and tree is viewed equally as God. This oversimplifies the case tremendously. Yogananda said that God is the "ocean" of all reality, but the individual waves are the infinitude of objects in the creation. I can say that "God has become me" but I cannot say

---

* Matt 6:8

† In this we need not quote St. John of the Cross or Saint Teresa but that greatest of theologians, Thomas Aquinas, who a year before his death had a mystical vision in which the formless Christ praises Thomas for his writings and asks him what he would like in return. "None other than Thyself, Lord" was his reply. He never wrote another word and considered his life's work "of little value."

"I am God."* Rocks presumably haven't realized their sonship with the Father, but Christ-like saints have. The rest of us are in varying degrees of Self-awareness. The gospel of John famously affirms our potential, "and as many as received Him to them gave He the power to become the sons of God."†

The Trinity Step-by-Step

To summarize: In the process of creation, we have the first stage wherein God, the Infinite Spirit, complete unto Itself, and the primary cause of all creation, moves a portion of consciousness with the intention to create. Movement produces vibration and vibration produces sound waves (and light waves). The etheric sound, soundless to ordinary human hearing, is described down through ages in various terms such as *AUM*, Amen, Amin, Ahunavar or the "music of the spheres." It is the primordial and pure (virginal) beginning. It is the "Word" as words form in the mind before being spoken; it is the mother of creation, and it contains all things that were made. Attuning our consciousness to it is deeply comforting and hence Jesus called it the Comforter. It is holy, and being invisible, it is ghost-like (like a wind or an invisible force) and brings to one all knowledge because out of it come all things.

As this cosmic wind moves, it produces a cosmic sound and begins to differentiate into a multiplicity of objects by

---

* This teaching that God has *become* all things doesn't change the reality that some people, some places, and some objects are holy while most other things, unaware of their true nature and asleep to divine awareness, are profane. This is true throughout the world, East and West. All things in creation have a subjective and an objective reality. The creation's existential dilemma is the separation of consciousness from form.

† John 1:12

the different rates of vibration. But it doesn't do this without intention or thought.

This innate and indwelling intention and intelligence is, like all thought, invisible, but unlike the movement of the "Word", which transforms into outward form, it remains invisible. Relative to the Father beyond and un-touched by creation, it is the only reflection of the Father that exists within the creation. It is therefore the "only be-gotten of the Father" (to be found within creation). It is the intelligent designer that makes it possible for an infinity of objects, including subtle objects such as thoughts and emotions, as well as actions, energy, and substance, to per-petuate themselves.

Vibration and Duality

As my thought becomes manifest in my speech and as that idea guides my actions toward the material and visible manifes-tation of my idea, so too, the vibration of God-consciousness stirs the void with waves of ever-increasing intensity. The speed or motion of the movement produces the appearance of objects. If the motion ceases, the objects disappear like quantum particles disappearing.

The simile of a pendulum is sometimes used to describe the function of duality and levels of manifestation from sub-tle to gross. The range of motion at the top of a pendulum is far less than the distance covered at the bottom of the pen-dulum. The higher up on the pendulum the more subtle or etheric is the manifestation. In this way there are varying degrees of subtlety or visible appearance. Not only do all physical objects in our world eventually decay and disappear, but our thoughts, far more subtle than physical objects, can vanish as quickly as they appear in our minds. So far as the world we inhabit during the day is concerned, that world disappears when we sleep.

Stare at an object for a long enough time and you find that the object disappears. It is the same with smell, touch, or taste. The experience of objects as separate from us requires constant motion. In part this is because visible objects are in fact merely vortices of vibrating particles of matter and energy. They appear separate only because we, as observers, vibrate differently than the objects in our field of observation.*

Genesis and Yogananda

In the Old Testament God says "Be still and know I AM. . . ."† In deep meditation when we turn within, the outer world fades to the background and can disappear altogether. Taking poetic license, when the music of creation ceases, the one left standing without a chair sees the Face of God. (The others fall asleep in their chairs.)

Although Yogananda focused mostly on Jesus' words in the New Testament, he did write about Genesis, the book of the Creation. In Genesis 1:2 we read "and the Spirit of God moved upon the face of the waters." In Yogananda's writings he describes this movement of God in terms of the primordial, or initial and sustaining, vibration, or wind of Spirit out

---

* To make matters worse, what we see, smell, taste, touch, or hear is experienced vicariously through the nervous system as the brain translates the vibratory impulses and molecules of the senses into what to us is a coherent and separate object. It's all in our head, as "they" say!

† Isaiah 46:10

of which energy and matter appear. The term "primordial" refers to creation's elemental stages before the infinitude of discrete objects comes into being. On an energy level, this primordial, intelligent vibration underlies all objects in creation even if it is not visible or detectable in a sensory way or by scientific instruments. It is both first in time (history) but also in essence.

The very first sentence in Genesis simply declares that God made heaven and earth. Yogananda describes "Heaven" as the invisible universe of energy* while "earth" is all that is visible. The movement of the Spirit of God is the vibration of God's consciousness in the initial act and intention to create. Just as the spoken word is an audible manifestation of the thought that precedes it and expresses the intention to act, this movement is the "Word" of God. Take note that Genesis repeats the phrase "and God said" with each act of creation. "Saying" means to speak and to speak is to say a "Word." The Word is the vibration of God's intention to create. The Word vibrates into existence the "waters" — the second stage of creativity for which Yogananda uses the term "energy." Energy of varying degrees of subtlety constitutes the fluid elements which immediately precede the appearance of visible things. We could call it the energetic or atomic building blocks of creation, or, in the ancient and classic term, the "elements."†

---

* Perhaps including "dark energy" or "dark matter"?

† The classic concept of elements were ether, air, fire, water, and earth. Quantum physics explores the energetic or vibratory underpinnings of the appearance of solid matter. It is here that science and metaphysics meet at last.

Thought, Energy, and Matter—Stages of Creation and Creativity

God's initial creative act is echoed in the ordinary human experience of creativity. As discussed earlier, I typically say, "I had a thought" but it would be more correct to say, "A thought came to me." If this thought produces a spark of enthusiasm in me, I begin planning how to manifest this new idea. With what is often a great deal of preparation and hard work I may, at last, manifest my idea. Thus, creativity passes through three stages: first, the idea; second, the energetic and creative response to the idea; and third, the effort to manifest the idea into form.*

The creation consists, therefore, of the invisible (consciousness) and the visible (all else that is measurable). The visible realm divides into two additional parts: the subtle and the obvious. The chemical, electrical, and atomic elements of matter are subtle (but measurable) while the manifesting object which appears to our sense of sight is the obvious. These three together parallel the three stages of creativity described above: idea, energy, and form. Energy is the link between consciousness and matter. In *Sanatan Dharma*† it is said that God *becomes* the world, but we might consider that in the process God, as pure Consciousness, is also veiled or hidden by the visible or measurable aspects of energy and form. But, as we've already established, being invisible doesn't mean nonexistent.

---

* Creativity is manifested in all three stages. Sometimes the final product is very different than the initial idea.

† *Sanatan Dharma* is the indigenous Sanskrit term for what later was called the basic teachings of Hinduism.

The three stages of creation described above form the basis for the terminology found in *Sanatan Dharma* that describes the ideational universe, the astral universe, and the physical cosmos. Taking this further into the microcosm of specific objects, including the human body, each object has three levels of existence, or "bodies": a body of thought (consciousness), energy, and form.

Returning to The Trinity: The Same, East and West

It will surprise most Christians if I now reveal that India's rishis also taught that there are three "persons" in God: The Holy Trinity. Although Christians limit the "son of God" to the personhood of Jesus Christ, it is relevant to this description of how God became the universe to describe a larger scope for the concept of "son of God."

Yogananda termed the visible vibratory creation (from the smallest atom to the largest object) the Holy Ghost. By contrast, the invisible indwelling divine intelligence he called the Christ consciousness of God. Thus the "son of God" is the divine consciousness hidden in and by the outward form of creation, while the outward form of creation is the vibration of Spirit manifesting appearances. God thus separated consciousness (which cannot be seen) from its outward form (which can be seen).

But WHY Did God Make Us?

The son of God is the offspring: the intention and impulse of God to manifest and perpetuate the creation. Who can say what motivated God to create? Theologians insist that God, to be God, could not have been under any compulsion to create. In the East it is said that God's motivation is described as a "desireless desire." This explanation sounds vaguely suspicious, I grant you, but imagine a day off when you have many choices on how to spend a beautiful, sunny spring day. You are not under any compulsion to do anything specifically, but you do have choices: all equally good. Or imagine yourself brimming with happiness. Are you going to stay home and hide or are you going to go out and be with friends?

We Are Made in the Image of God

As the paintings of an artist tend to reflect the style and perhaps the attitude of the artist, the creation reflects the signature and fingerprint of the Creator. Whatever the motive for God's act of creation, we, made by necessity in the divine image, are imprinted with a similar creative impulse and with the concomitant intelligence to use it. All things seem to have the impulse and ability to sustain their existence, directly or through procreation. As any act of creativity brings satisfaction, joy, or pleasure to its creator, we can imagine that in so doing we experience a tiny fraction of the bliss of God, the ultimate Creator. The invisible but omnipresent intelligence in nature, in creation, is the "son" or reflection of the Father, at least in the cosmic or macro sense of the Trinity.

Holy Ghost Vibration

Creation is a "ghost" for the reasons of its innate insubstantiality, meaning its inherent illusory nature, according both to ancient metaphysics and now even to modern science. It is "holy" in the sense that it is an emanation of God-consciousness in the initial vibrational energy (like the big bang, so to speak) out of which all seemingly separate objects appear. It is also the "Mother" because it is this initial "Word" or vibration of God consciousness that is its immediate source. As described earlier, it is the "Word" because we are referencing the initial, or primordial, vibration of God consciousness that "is the beginning." Because all things have their sustaining source in the Holy Word or Divine Mother vibration, it is said to be the Comforter, like being in the womb, for those who "hear" its voice. By our inner attunement with it, it brings to our remembrance all things that are true because it is the source of all things. All vibration and motion produce waves in the vast spectrum of sound, light, and electromagnetism. This holy vibration is said to produce a sacred sound. The sound has been given different names down through time and history, names such as amen, *AUM*, Ahunavar, Hum, and Amin.

Only Son of God?

Returning to the "son of God," we come to the crossroads of East and West: *Sanatan Dharma* and Christianity. Christian theology states that Jesus Christ, a human being, was the "*only* begotten son of God." Who was Jesus Christ? Was Jesus *a* son of God or *the* son of God? Yogananda and the teachings of the rishis of India maintain that the "son of God" is the intelligence and intention of God hidden invisibly in the visible creation, and that any individual soul who, by a combination of effort and grace, achieves realization and oneness of Spirit and Nature, uniting consciousness with the forms of creation, becomes a Self-realized son of God. As the Trinity is One, the oneness includes oneness with the Father as well as unity of the son and Holy Ghost.

Thus, John the Apostle could write in the opening chapter that "As many as received him, to them gave he the power to become the sons of God."* In Genesis, we see two references to the sons of God.† We see references to "sons" (plural) in the Book of Job and in the letters to the Philippians and the Romans.‡

Thus, in the Eastern view, "son of God" refers to both the macrocosmic existence of divine intelligence in created things, and to the realization of this consciousness in the consciousness of a Self-realized and incarnate human being such as Jesus, Buddha, and Krishna. In addition, as this potential exists especially in the consciousness of humans, there can be many sons of God, both simultaneously and in history. This is both our soul's origin and our destiny, provided we, like the prodigal son, make the conscious choice to return home.

So, you see, the only true reality is God alone: whether in form, in thought, or transcendent of both. We, too, are triune beings in thought, feeling, and form.

The Bridge Over the River That Divides East from West

This, then, is the bridge that can connect East and West. As the Jews of Jesus' time could not accept that he was a son of God, so the Christians of the modern era seem, as yet,

---

* John 1:12; *see also*: John 14:12 "Verily, verily, I say unto you, He that believeth on me, the works that I do shall he do also; and greater works than these shall he do; because I go unto my Father." And Matt 16:25 "Whosoever shall seek to save his life shall lose it; and whosoever shall lose his life for my sake [that is, merge his life in God] shall find it."

† Genesis 6:2,4

‡ See references to "sons of God" in Genesis 6:1–4; 1 John 3:13; Romans 8:13–15; Philippians 2:14–16.

unaware that we too have that same potential. From this realization comes the knowing that all creation contains within it the seed of divine consciousness, for God alone is the substance of all creation. For those with ears to hear and eyes to see, this truth is inextricably woven throughout both the Old and New Testaments. As our world integrates at an increasingly rapid pace, the time has come for this truth to free us, especially Christians, from the more limited understanding of Jesus Christ. "Who do men say I AM?"

Recap the Trinity

To dial back to the subject of the triune nature of God we have these three: 1) God beyond creation, 2) God AS creation, and 3) God within creation. *Sanatan Dharma* states that the Infinite Spirit divides into the Trinity in the initial act of creation. First, the Spirit becomes God the Father who remains beyond and untouched by creation;* second, the Holy Ghost is the "breath" of God: that energetic movement (or vibration) which brings into visible form the objects of creation; and third, God's intelligence and intention lie invisibly hidden at the still-center of that vibration, residing motionless at the heart of every atom, yet functioning to guide that object in its purpose and form.

The Holy Family

Another way the Eastern teachings describe this is to say that the Word is the "consort" of the Father, or the

---

* In India, the Christian Trinity is known by the mantric sounds or syllables: *Sat, Tat, AUM* (usually spoken or written in reverse as *AUM, Tat, Sat*). *Sat* is the Father, *Tat* is the Son, and *AUM* is the Holy Ghost. See the book of poems, Paramhansa Yogananda, "Demand to the Holy Trinity," *Whispers from Eternity* (California: Crystal Clarity Publishers, 2008), #100.

co-creator or Mother of creation. The metaphor generated by this description is that of the Holy Family: The Father, who remains apart from the creation (like dad who goes off to work every day), impregnates the consort-Mother (the Holy Ghost) with the seed of God's intention to create. This seed intelligence is the "son" (a reflection of the Father). It has no form or body but exists as intention and intelligence at the still-point of all motion. It is the true "son of God" immanent in all creation. It reflects the blissful, ever-perfect, completely still Spirit just as a son might bear a resemblance to his father.

Christ Consciousness

Paramhansa Yogananda called this indwelling and re-flected consciousness of God the "Christ consciousness." It is immanent in all creation and thus is said to be universal. This does not deny the sonship of God declared by Jesus Christ, Lord Krishna and other great world saviors. What this posits is that the "I" spoken of by Jesus and other saviors is the uni-versal Christ consciousness as it is manifested in, though not limited to, a particular human form. This universal Christ consciousness, in whatever form, is always "one with the Father." But in the God-sent savior, the Christ consciousness is fully Self-realized while in most humans it is not yet so.

AUM Vibration

The "Word," or Holy Ghost, or *AUM* vibration is the motor, or engine, one might say, of creation. As pointed out previously, this vibration emits a sound, and this sound, which can be heard by anyone, has various names in the different spiritual traditions. Names such as the Amen, the Amin, the Ahunavar, the Hum, or the *AUM* sound. The vibration of the cosmic motor has within itself three separate rates of vibrations consonant with its three-fold task to manifest creation: a higher pitched sound that represents the process of creating; a mid-range sound representing the act of sustaining; and a lower sound representing the act of dissolving. In Hinduism, these three functions of the cosmic sound of *AUM* are personified as Brahma, Vishnu, and Shiva (Creator, Preserver, and Destroyer).

The *AUM* sound can be heard inside the right ear in meditation, or in a quiet place, and sometimes it is heard audibly without meditation or effort. In most, if not all spiritual traditions, prayers begin and/or end with the holy and sacred sound (*AUM*, Amen, etc.) in hopes that the prayer is sown into the ether of Truth and will become manifest.[*]

Listening to its sacred vibration in meditation serves as the witness of the ever-present, immanent but silent divinity, the blissful Christ consciousness. Just as the sound of a car's motor tells us the motor is running, the hum of *AUM* assures us of God's indwelling presence. As the vast starry night sky represents, for many people, the invisible hand of the Creator; so inner communion with the *AUM* or Amen vibration brings comfort and joy to the meditator, knowing that one is in contact with divine realms.

The *AUM* vibration (or Holy Ghost, Comforter, or Word) is said to be pure and thus a "virgin" because as the origin

---

[*] The yogis say, and great saints aver, that light is the higher octave or vibration of sound. Here, however, I have chosen to focus on sound. In fact, Yogananda taught that the Holy Ghost vibration of *AUM* manifests eight distinct attributes which can be experienced by the devotee: peace, wisdom, energy, love, calmness, sound, light, and bliss.

of all things it is not yet tainted by the differentiation that follows. It is like a stem cell in the body in its original state which has not yet divided itself into a multiplicity of organs. As stated earlier, the leading edge of science is moving in the direction of paralleling the ancient teaching of *Sanatan Dharma*: that all objects consist of energy. It seems to me that the outermost boundary of science will be found when energy appears to dissolve into or appear out from "nothing." This "nothing" is what metaphysics posits as consciousness. No instrument or mathematical equation can limit or define consciousness. Consciousness is cognized only by consciousness. But such investigations and conclusions are yet in the future, and I can thus only speculate.[*]

In any case, science, it has been said by others more knowledgeable than me, is beginning to resemble a page from the hoary Vedas of India. The Vedas declare that matter is an illusion requiring a Seer (consciousness), the means of seeing (using the mind and its connection to functioning senses), and an object of sight. Science states that the observer cannot be separated from the observation and its results.[†]

---

[*] We can see the consequences of consciousness in one who speaks, moves, or breathes. But the signs of consciousness are not the same as consciousness itself.
[†] One of the most bizarre findings of science is the impact of the observer on the results of an experiment. "Quantum Theory Demonstrated: Observation Affects Reality," Weizmann Institute of Science.

Chapter 4

Fall from Grace

Why Do We Not "See" God?

T HE TRUE AND PURE NATURE OF DIVINE INTELLI-
gence within all things is masked from us and all
objects in at least two ways. First, most objects in
creation are not yet self-aware. Second, most humans,
though possessing the potential for self-awareness, are mostly preoccupied with using this intelligence for material gain
and ego affirmation or protection. Because the outer form
of creation is in constant motion while the invisible intelligence of creation is still and silent, all too often it seems
that "never the twain shall meet."* Reuniting these two is
one way of describing the spiritual path. Humans, because
we retain some of the memory of being in lower life forms,
are habituated to being preoccupied with survival and
procreation and are not yet accustomed to being silently
reflective. Interestingly, Patanjali, the author of the *Yoga
Sutras*, describes the path to enlightenment in terms of our
remembering, which in Sanskrit, he writes as *smriti*.†

* From Rudyard Kipling's poem, "The Ballad of East and West."
† In the parable of the Prodigal Son, he "remembers" what it was like in his father's

Why Suffering? Why Evil? Our Choice?

The complexity of created things stems in part from the ceaseless play of opposites such as positive and negative, good and evil, and pleasure and pain. These have their origins in the one ingredient necessary for the great drama of creation to work independently and creatively: choice, or free will. God's initial choice to create the universe set into motion the pattern and usefulness of choice as the agent of creation. In *Sanatan Dharma* it is said that like the Garden of Eden in Genesis, God initially created the universe as a place of beauty and harmony.

But without endowing the creatures with any choice in the matter except the opportunity to enjoy the beauty and then, seeing it for what it was — a dream of the Creator — what else could they do but merge back into the Creator? Thus, the drama couldn't continue.

One version given humanity by way of a story is that some to whom God commissioned the details of creation became attached to the creation and to their control over it. Wanting to "play God," these rebellious angels, led by one called Lucifer, decided to take matters in their own hands. Or so the story goes.

But look around you. Look within you! Would most people want it any other way? Aren't most people busy with their ambitions, dreams, hopes, fears, and hurts? Isn't it really you and I who want to have life on our terms? Isn't it we who have our own desires and opinions on the questions of life? And isn't it reasonable to describe this impulse as our wanting to "play God"?*

home. In the story of the "Prince and the Pauper," the prince, thinking he was but a pauper, reawakens to his royal lineage.

* Ironically, it would seem to some that God, having set the rules of creation into motion, generally plays by those rules and doesn't get to "play God."

Memory of Perfection

Returning now to the story: after turning their backs on God and coming up with a scheme to perpetuate the creation, these fallen angels began creating patterns of disease, imperfection, and death. Yogananda commented that reincarnation became the means for human souls, who, being made in the image of God, were accustomed to beauty and perfection, to come back to fix things that were "wrong." Being thus focused on the various shortcomings and imperfections of the outer world, these originally sanctified first-humans forgot that these too were simply part of God's dream of creation.

These first creatures, the Adam and the Eve of humanity, were enticed by that same temptation to "play God" and eat of the fruit of the tree of knowledge of good and evil. Before we consider the Garden of Eden in greater detail, it would be natural to ask whether God failed to foresee this unfortunate turn of events. Being God, how could this have been a surprise?

It would make sense that the creation, being a manifestation of God, would possess some of the procreative impulse and intelligence of God. What would be the point if God ends up being a micro-manager? The endowment of divine intelligence as a seed in the womb of the creation is one way — from a macrocosmic view — to understand the statement from the Bible that "God so loved the world that He gave to the world his only-begotten son."

Maya — *Illusion*

In India a complementary story exists that says when God saw that the creatures were enjoying the creation for a time but then merging back into Bliss it was obvious that the creation would not last very long. God saw that the creation would need to seem more real and its inherent, dream-like nature would have to be obscured further. The divine outgoing force of vibration and duality was consequently "ramped up" to make it more difficult to pierce the veil of illusion, known in Sanskrit as *maya*. This illusion proved to be our undoing as we have become identified and attached to the *maya* of creation. It's only a story, but it's one at "our expense" to be sure.

One can hardly imagine that God failed to see what was coming but, there you have it.

A further question arises: is humankind essentially good or essentially evil? The doctrine of Original Sin seems to suggest the latter: it states that we are evil by our own natural impulses and due to the past transgressions of Adam and Eve. Yet Genesis states that we are made "in the image of God."[*] We must therefore have some redeeming qualities or potential. Which is it? Let's reach for our guiding mantra: "Both-And". Let me tease you with one significance of the teaching that God "became" the creation: the "dice are loaded."

[*] Genesis 1:26, 27

Chapter 5

Garden of Eden

THE HUMAN BODY, YOGANANDA TAUGHT, HAS BEEN created intentionally by God to be able to experience non-duality, bliss, or God as the *summum bonum* and the purpose of God's creation. As illustrated in the story of the Garden of Eden, it is God's wish that we enjoy the creation with God — in the state of bliss and constant communion with the Creator. It is not God's intention that we must shed the human form, to die as we view it, before we can meet our Maker and enjoy the heaven of bliss that is our home and our destiny. Jesus himself declared that "The kingdom of heaven is not 'Lo here,' or 'Lo there,' but within you."*

The rebellion against remaining in the Eden of God consciousness evidently occurred among both angels and men. The rebellion at the higher level sowed the seeds for objective imperfections, while our individual, human attraction or repulsion to *maya* accounts for our personal forgetfulness of Spirit.†

---

* Luke 17:20–21
† In the Garden of Eden story in Genesis, Satan's rebellion had already occurred.

This is how and why we read the stories of the fallen angels who rebelled during the process of creation and how it is, thereafter, more personally and individually, that Satan appears in the form of the snake in the Garden of Eden; as the tester in the Book of Job; as the tempter of Jesus in the desert; and in the lives of saints like St. Anthony of the Desert; or in the twentieth century, the life of Padre Pio, the stigmatic of southern Italy.

Satan is a conscious, formerly angelic (and therefore powerfully creative) force, and as such holds all things separate from one another. The satanic force had been commissioned to create all things but rebelled, as described above, drunk with creative power.* This force became identified with the things it had created and viewed them, analogous to God in Genesis describing the creation "as good," as worthy of "worship."† The satanic force decided that it no longer wanted to co-create in harmony with the original intention of God.

The creation and its indwelling intelligence have been hijacked, as it were, to see itself as an end not merely a means, of finding happiness. Whether by pride, ignorance, indifference, or the influence of this "mayic" or satanic matter-bound consciousness, we humans made (and continue to make) a similar choice. We seek happiness outside ourselves, in the world of matter and the sense-driven ego. We "worship" the "idols" of pleasure, power, wealth, name, fame, and possessions. The pattern of choosing the means to an end as an end in itself is the classic case of "missing the point."‡

---

* Considering human history, how often do we see rulers "drunk with power?"

† Genesis 1:3; Matt 4:9: Satan told Jesus that he, Jesus, could have dominion over all the world if he would but worship him (Satan).

‡ *Yoga Sutras of Patanjali* describes one of the obstacles to spiritual growth as "missing the point." Sutras Book 1:30

Satan, as a conscious force, need not personally
bother with most people because most are not seeking
God-realization. Satan only appears to the likes of Buddha,
Jesus, and great saints on the eve of their ascension into cosmic consciousness. "He" does so to stir the memories of their
former desires. Satan can take a human or animal form just
as a Self-realized soul, one with the Father, can do. This is
not to say the satanic force is equal to God or to the soul
as a son of God, but only that this creative formerly angelic
force can take on the appearance of anything in the vibratory
creation that it has worked so hard to create for its own sake.*

Desire, it is said, is the downfall of the wise.† In
Yogananda's life story, he shares personal stories of his guru's
youth including one in which his guru, as a child, became
enamored of an "ugly dog belonging to a neighbor. I kept my
household in turmoil for weeks to get that dog. My ears were
deaf to offers of pets with more prepossessing appearance.
Moral: Attachment is blinding; it lends an imaginary halo of
attractiveness to the object of desire."

In an archetypal but all too real sense, we make that
choice when we lose the innocence of childhood and enter
puberty. Our "nakedness," our separateness (and not just
sexual polarity), and our egoity begin to take shape, form,
and individual initiative.

Sanatan Dharma depicts Satan in metaphysical rather
than anthropomorphic terms. The terms used include ignorance (rather than sin) and delusion (or *maya*). The explanation given by Yogananda is also more impersonal and
macrocosmic. It goes something like this: the outflowing

* Thus, Satan took on the form of jackals and other animals in the temptations
of St. Antony of the desert.
† Bhagavad Gita 3:37

Word of God (Holy Ghost/Divine Mother) reaches a point where, being conscious, it begins to detach from looking back to God or inward to the Christ intelligence for direction but darts on ahead on its own to create patterns and objects. It is a conscious force and operates both on the macrocosmic level creating disease, germs, harmful animals, etc., and the microcosmic level tempting those who are temptable (my new word, take note) to revel or suffer in the creation as a separate reality from God. (Example: a person who is inclined to want something for nothing is more likely to fall for a con than one who is content with what he has and what he can obtain by his own effort.) It is we who invite ourselves into either the consciousness of wisdom or desire.

There is a story of Yogananda meeting a Christian minister. The minister was of the mind to take every word of the Bible literally. So, when, in their conversation, Yogananda asked this man about that snake in the Garden of Eden who evidently talked to Adam and Eve, the minister replied that "In those days snakes could talk!" Yogananda removed his hat with a sweeping gesture saying to the man, "I bow to the temple of ignorance I behold before me."

In Yogananda's now famous life story, *Autobiography of a Yogi*, he relates how his guru, Swami Sri Yukteswar, gave him a more intelligible explanation of the Garden of Eden story. In this explanation, our "parents" (Adam and Eve) were tempted away from the bliss of God's presence by the memory, retained from prior lifetimes in animal forms, of sexual union.*

---

* Not unlike stories such as the virgin birth of Jesus, it is an ancient memory or truth, Yogananda wrote, that at one time humanity's state of divine consciousness was so great that children could be conceived and born by willpower and did not require reproduction by sexual means.

Tree of Life

In the teachings of India, the human body is referred to as an upturned tree. In the Bible there are also references to the Tree (or River) of Life. In India, it is described as an upturned tree with its roots (the hair, or more correctly, the energies of the brain and mind) above and its branches (arms and legs and nervous system) below.* The sexual function is said to be in the center of the garden and Adam and Eve were told by God not to indulge in its fruit (the sense of touch and the subconscious memory of sexual union).†

Procreation via sexual means is said to be second only to the compelling urge for self-preservation. As the means of perpetuating the great drama of life, it makes some sense that this creative impulse, as described above in the macrocosm of the Satanic force, would be the first impulse in the assertion of personal separation and independence from God. With procreation we play being God the creator.

In the words of the story itself, Adam and Eve are tempted to eat the fruit of the tree of *knowledge* of good and evil.‡ One might object to the interpretation that sex was their downfall since it would appear from the language of Genesis that knowledge was the temptation. I think it advisable not to get too stuck on a word like knowledge. It seems that Yogananda did not want to dissect Genesis unnecessarily. I conclude that what is meant in the story is that Adam and Eve were not content to remain in the garden of divine consciousness but were tempted to experience the illusions offered by *maya*.

* Rig Veda mantra I.164.20; Bhagavad Gita 15:1

† Genesis 2:17; 3:13

‡ Genesis 4:1 "Adam *knew* Eve his wife." Here the word "know" is used to refer to sex. Whatever the etymology or interpretation, it IS an interesting coincidence.

Accepting the term knowledge, we might add that divine knowledge is the experience that God is the underlying reality of all created things. Adam and Eve initially lived in the consciousness of all things as divine manifestations. Their nakedness, for example, meant nothing special to them. But, with the prompting of the serpent of sex memory, they demonstrated their preference for the dual vision in which all things, male and female included, are seen as separate and desirable. The fact that the story states that their lack of awareness of their nakedness prior to temptation was followed by the donning of animal skins after their temptation certainly suggests an important consequence, if not motivation, for their choice.

Where was the Garden of Eden?

Yogananda's esoteric interpretation of this story that the garden was not a place in the Middle East but that it is a reference to the human body makes far more sense than a literal garden on planet Earth. Whether literal or not, the story still holds water as a metaphor.*

Reason and Feeling

Yogananda describes Eve as representing the feeling element in human consciousness and Adam as the thinking or perceptive element. This separation is inherent in achieving the appearance of the creation because the

---

* Genesis seems to go out of its way to describe the location of the Garden identifying the Tigris and Euphrates Rivers as having their source in the Garden. This could easily be interpreted allegorically, however. In fact, in yogic lore the two "rivers" are the subtle astral channels of *ida* and *pingala*. But this goes beyond the purpose of this book.

consciousness behind the appearance of form or an act can either be divine or satanic, so to speak (non-dual or dual). As stated earlier, the very act of creation entailed separating consciousness from form. In the esoterica of metaphysics, the "Eve" (feeling) is the Holy Ghost vibration which produces the appearance of form while the "Adam" is equivalent to the son of God (Christ or Krishna) consciousness or perception. Feeling is associated with vibration because its very nature is that of motion. Feelings or emotions are vibrations that come and go. Reason or perception is associated with stillness because the act of perception is relatively motionless and as our thoughts are private, so consciousness is invisible to outward sight. Both are equal partners as manifestations of God. Uniting the two is the goal of the soul in creation.

What, then, might be this *knowledge* that Adam and Eve, and by extension, each one of us seeks? It is the desire, as has often been stated by spiritual writers, to be like God; to be independent; to see the world with all its ups and downs as real, as good (or evil), apart and independent from God; and yes, to create our own world, sexually, of course, but in many other ways such as possessions, wealth, power over others, security, fame, and recognition.

So "Eve," representing our feeling aspect, succumbs to the temptation of independence, of power, of sex desire, and creativity and convinces the "Adam" of our reason that to have this freedom on our own is a good and worthy goal. Who then is this rascal, the snake? Why couldn't the two of them have been tempted and made the decision to eat the apple on their own? Why did they need the snake?

Who was the Snake in the Garden?

On general principles, and in the reflected light of Yogananda's explanation, the presence of the snake conveys several important truths. Let me give a few examples below:

Evil or ignorance is not our nature. The tempting force is outside our true nature. The delusive force or consciousness is ignorant of, or forgetful of, or rebellious against, the true, divine nature of God in creation. In fact, the dice of reality are loaded in favor of our eventual return to God because we are made in the image of God. The snake symbolizes an illusion, a non-real force relative to the sole reality of God. It is not who we are.

What is the nature of delusion? This non-real force is called *maya* in *Sanatan Dharma* and Satan in Christian dogma. It is the outward flowing energy and intelligence of God that turns its back on its divine origins and sets up shop in the creation as its own, ostensibly separate reality.

The snake or dragon symbol is universal. Curiously, the personification of the snake as delusion in the case of Adam and Eve is essentially the same as it is in India and China: that of a serpent or dragon. But in *Sanatan Dharma*, the serpent force has a dual nature: either as temptress or savior and is personified as a goddess with the name *Kundalini*.

Kundalini. In yoga teachings, *Kundalini* is an energy force that is coiled tightly at the base of the human spine in the energy (astral) body. Jesus himself said, "The kingdom of God is within you."* In its coiled form it represents our soul's choice to "eat the fruit of the tree of the knowledge of good

* Luke 17:21

and evil." In short, the soul's choice to rebel. But when the soul, like the prodigal son, remembers its divine nature it calls *Kundalini* to rise from its lair and move upward to the seat of the soul at the top of the head.*

The serpent's dual nature in Christianity. In the Christian narrative, the dual nature of the serpent is somewhat obscured but nonetheless present "for those with eyes to see." When, in Genesis, Eve is beguiled by the serpent and partakes of the apple, God addresses the serpent saying, "I will put enmity between you and the woman."† The serpent is thus juxtaposed to the "woman" as enemies but also opposites. This comes full circle in Revelations, the last book of the Bible, when the dragon confronts a "woman clothed in the sun." In both Genesis and Revelations, the context relates to the pain associated with childbirth. In Revelations, the child is assumed to be the Christ, the redeemer.

Moses and the serpent. In the book of Numbers, Moses is commanded by God to make a serpent of brass and to set it upon a pole and anyone who was bitten by a desert serpent would be healed by looking upon the brass serpent.‡ The apostle John wrote that as Moses lifted up the serpent, even so must the son of Man be lifted up in order to receive eternal life.§ We can't really believe that gazing upon a brass serpent would heal one from a snake bite. Adding to John's quote from the Old Testament about lifting up the son of man, we

---

* In the eastern tradition, the dragon guards a great treasure: the secret of our immortality. Only one pure of heart can slay the dragon: "Blessed are the pure of heart for they shall see God." Matt 5:9

† Genesis 3:15

‡ Numbers 21:8–9

§ John 3:14–15

can perhaps understand Yogananda's interpretation that the serpent spoken of is the *Kundalini* or serpent power. When *Kundalini* rises, or is lifted up, we are cured from the bite of delusion and this lifting up from egoity to soul consciousness is the process of awakening that leads to eternal life.*

By now I think you'll agree that the Adam and Eve story has more going for it than the ridiculous idea of a talking snake. The choice Adam and Eve made is the choice every adolescent makes, and the choice adults make every day. That our "first parents" made this decision and we have inherited its consequences seems quite obviously unfair, but perhaps we are our own "first parents" and we too, in our first appearance in human form, made the same decision just as we continue to do every day. This means most people are busy pursuing the will-o'-the-wisp desires that make the world go around — and they do so in earnest. As Swami Kriyananda put it, "Most people wouldn't have it any other way." Most people do not go to "heaven" because for them it would be "hell" because they are too eager for the rewards of the senses. They are not peaceful in themselves. God doesn't talk to most people, Yogananda said, because most would argue with him.

The Garden of Eden: Allegory or Fact?

Yogananda did not dismiss the Adam and Eve story as just an allegory. Depending on which of his writings you discover, his reference might sound literal, like that of a Christian fundamentalist, or in other contexts, wholly allegorical. My conclusion is that there are some teachings on which he seemed to be, perhaps purposely, vague. As we will see later in the

---

* Yogananda explained that Jesus' term, son of man, is a reference to the body-bound ego. Son of God refers to the soul.

discussion of Jesus' views on reincarnation, Yogananda, too, couldn't say everything because those to whom he came to help couldn't accept "everything." Think of parents and their relationship to their children. It is very similar. You cannot say or disclose many things about human life to young children. Even between adults there are topics that are not spoken of, out of respect or out of what is right and proper.

Garden of Eden: From a Higher Age?

A prevailing concept in the great civilizations of ancient times is the idea that there was "once upon a time" when humans were wise, harmonious and in tune with God. Even the Adam and Eve story suggests as much. An excellent book for those with the courage to consider a rewrite of human history is called *The Yugas*. I will touch on this in a later chapter. But the idea of a golden past, a higher civilization, lurks in the creation stories of perhaps all cultures. Those who study the history of the earth and humanity are still searching for evidence of the great flood which is found in storytelling from all over the planet. The existence of higher civilizations is accumulating more evidence every year. My personal view on the Adam and Eve story is that it has its genesis (pun intended) in the story of man's fall from a higher age of consciousness.

Will We Find the "Missing Link"?

During Yogananda's life in America (1920–1952), the teaching of evolution was a hot item. I suppose it still is. Yogananda stated that humanity would never find "the missing link." He stated plainly that the human form, not unlike the literal story of Genesis, was a "special" creation, a conscious act of creation by God. Is there a role for aliens here? I don't know and it really doesn't matter. If aliens came and seeded the human form, it would still beg the question of how the aliens evolved.

Yogananda conceded, whether for the purposes of avoiding further discussion or otherwise, that the human body must have evolved to some degree from lower forms. But he insisted the human body did not evolve through the blind, instinctual action of forces of natural (or random) selection. He insisted God stepped in to make "man" as it were from the dust of the earth by breathing life into the nostrils of the first "man."

I've long felt unsatisfied by this for one simple reason: how did it take place? Yogananda did not say, just as Genesis did not say, *how* God manifested creation. Yogananda insisted, just as Genesis portrayed it, that God reached down to earth and took a direct hand in things.

My personal view (and I don't need to stick with it) is that Yogananda was more focused on the need to address the consciousness and issues of his times, and indeed ours as well. It was important, I suspect, for him to state that the human body was an intentional creation designed to make it possible for the human being to achieve Self-realization. He was countering the thought, prevalent then and now, that natural and unconscious forces evolved, perhaps even accidentally or randomly, the human brain and nervous system. There is an entire culture that uses Darwin and other presumably scientific findings to aver that life, and especially human life, has no inherent meaning or purpose and that values are merely relative (perhaps to our personal convenience). I am not going to tackle this issue. Swami Kriyananda did so masterfully in a series of books.*

He also asserted as a fact that humans with higher, God-attuned consciousness could create children in the "immaculate" or non-sexual manner. This does evidently occur in nature at times but, once again, he did not give any background or explanation. We see this averred in the story of Jesus' birth and that also of Buddha. Yogananda did point out, however, that an immaculate birth is not necessary to signal the birth of the soul of a world savior. Why then does it exist? Yogananda did not say. It has at least the obvious symbolic message that this birth is of one of purity and divinity.†

In his teachings, therefore, he sticks to the basic story of Genesis though he commented that the six days of creation were not to be taken literally.

---

* *Out of the Labyrinth, God is for Everyone*, and *Hope for a Better World*. Crystal Clarity Publishers.

† In the teachings of all great civilizations that humanity at least once experienced a golden age of harmony and wisdom, it may well be that powers we would call "miraculous" were commonplace. Selbie and Steinmetz, *The Yugas*, 2010.

Chapter 6

But Why?

IT IS SAID THAT THE NATURE OF GOD IS BLISS ITSELF and that it is the nature of bliss to share that joy with others. If a wife announces that a planned pregnancy is successful, the happy couple celebrates by telling all their family and friends. When good things happen, or when we ourselves are in a happy and exuberant mood, we don't shut ourselves up in our room. We naturally go out "to play."

So, God, bliss incarnate, so to speak, bubbling over with contagious happiness has this desireless-desire to share that happiness with countless Beings, who like God, are made of the very same Bliss. God envisions a happy world, in other words. But if these sentient Beings are merely reproductions in the form of the formless Godhead, then they are but puppets, automatons. Such Beings will have been deprived of the free choice that God, as Bliss, had and used to begin with. The love and happiness of these Beings for God would therefore be false because they were imposed upon them by their nature and for which they have had no choice. God had a choice so why shouldn't those who God has created? Our wanting to be like God is based on the truth that we are made in the image of God. But it is our insistence that we do it "our way," separate from God's will, that is the cause of our troubles.

What would the experience of God's love be if the Beings of the universe were mere knockoffs of the Supreme Being, devoid of the choice to love? Free will — and thus individual independence — is the requisite price for an authentic choice to seek God, the source of Love and Bliss. God HAS every-thing; God IS every-thing. But God gives us the choice to seek that unconditional love and bliss when we are ready. Our decision to surrender our existential independence is a free will offering back to God. Our choice to remain separate from God is sufficiently attractive to us to have made that choice. To return the gift of this choice to God is truly an act of love only because God does not compel us to do so.

Why be surprised that the conscious creatures of creation, endowed with the very impulse to create and experience the thrill of creating, would want to be like the Creator? Creating things from babies to symphonies to entire galaxies and perhaps even universes is intoxicatingly "addictive" because creativity combines intense joy with an exhilarating sense of power and self-worth. It is therefore easy to imagine that these "early adaptors" became forgetful of the One who has given them life and purpose. Does not the son aspire to succeed like the father? Does a child not desire the inheritance sooner rather than later? Does not a son wish to accomplish even greater things than the father?*

---

* I ask the indulgence of those who squirm at the use of binary nouns and pronouns but sometimes it's just easier to flow with the metaphor (father and son, that is). The Infinite Spirit, God, has no gender; nor do our souls, made in the image of the Creator.

This, then, is the greatest story ever told. It is the great drama, or *lila* as it is said in Sanskrit, of God's creation. The Bible quote, "God so loved the world. . .," means more than a description of the birth, life, and death of Jesus Christ. God's son (the seed of intention to choose to create) lives in each atom of creation and, more importantly for you and me, in each one of us.

Chapter 7

Is the World but a Dream?

THE SUBJECT OF DUALITY LEADS US TO THE TEACHING of metaphysics and *Sanatan Dharma* that avers that the universe and all things and thoughts are naught but a dream of the Creator. I believe a previous Pope, or the Vatican issued a warning to young people that this Eastern teaching is insidious. I didn't research the encyclical or papal bull so I've only heard this from others but what scripture or religious worldview can be considered holy if it suggests irresponsibility in ethics and morals? I admit that such a teaching is not for everyone for the simple reason that, like the Vatican, not everyone will understand its meaning. Let me try, therefore, to elucidate this curious teaching from India.

The rishis of ancient India counseled their students to contemplate the experience of sleep. At night in the subconscious state of dreams, we experience the dream as real. We may run for our life in the dream from the bad people and then just as we are about to get the ax, we wake up in a cold sweat. Realizing that "it was just a dream" we lay back down and return to sleep.

The next morning, we wake up again. How many have

wondered, based on the experience of the dream state, whether the waking state is also but a dream? Is death but another change from one dream to another? There are many aspects of our waking life that have a dream-like quality. We go from being the loving "Daddy" at home to a mere cog in the grinding wheel of some factory or organizational chart. Or from being a harried mother at home to a smiling celebrity on the stage. In the morning we might sit silently with our aging and forgetful parent who scolds us for our inattentiveness while later that day, in the afternoon, we might be standing in a room barking orders to our attentive lieutenants.

God plays all the parts, it is said. This world is but a play, a divine *lila,* an amusement of God. Such statements are an exaggeration. God is no fool: God sees the suffering and feels the pangs of our longing. But what kind of drama would life be if it were always pleasant and nice? We'd probably do away with ourselves out of boredom. We'd also probably do away with ourselves if life were unending torture and violence. Quite apart from the conscious satanic, rebellious consciousness described earlier, the simple fact is that the show would not continue were it not a variety show. It could not hold our interest unless it weren't always changing, offering promises of fulfillment one moment and threatening potential disaster the next. If that relationship didn't work out, well, what about Sally over there? Or Jim? If you don't like working for Starbucks, try Amazon.

The world as a dream of God makes sense only if you are dreaming *with* God, *in* God-consciousness. For the rest of us, it can be all too real. With God, Yogananda said, life is joy; without God, it can be a nightmare. Of course, it isn't that extreme, is it?

From Shakespeare's play, *As You Like It*, from the mouth of Jaques: "All the world's a stage, and all the men and women merely players; they have their exits and their entrances, and one man in his time plays many parts. . . ."

The Great Playwright has written the drama of the ages. The A-grade actors play their parts according to the script. B-grade actors confuse their self-identity with the parts they play in the drama. The great actors and actresses can play a wide range of parts. The other kind get typecast, and in their daily life such actors begin to live out their stage persona. The great ones are not smitten with fortune or fame. They are just people like you and me. The best ones see the pangs and sufferings of others and use their prominence to help.

Our role is to play our part as well as we can knowing that even as we do that it is just a play. We may get a starring role or be someone's sidekick or maybe we're just a Joe or a Jane. But if we tune into the script of the Director we can say when the play is done "Well done, Lord! We had a jolly good time!"

I must add that we have an active role in the script. Just as an actor looks to the director for direction, but with skill brings the drama alive, so we should tune into divine guidance to do that which is ours to do.

Here's a punch list to wrap our heads around this dream concept:

1. When the Boogie Man is chasing you in your dreams, you are in great fright! During the dream, it is unquestionably real to you. Upon waking you realize it was "only a dream" and like our nightly dreams, I cannot say it is a dream until I have awakened from it.

2. No one is saying that the world we live in doesn't exist. We are simply saying that it isn't what it appears to be! (Isn't that what modern science is telling us?)

3. So long as we are caught up in the dream of life, the steps required to awaken from the dream are just as necessary and real to us as the dream itself. Thus, we must embark upon virtue, self-discipline, devotion, self-control, etc. etc. Goodness and virtue are, like everything else, vibrations and, as such, these vibrations are closer to exiting the dream than the vibrations of selfishness or evil. We might say that goodness and virtue are the cost of the exit visa from illusion to transcendence.*

4. There are at least two aspects of this dream of life: the objective world of the five senses and the subjective world in our head. As the objective world is infinitely complex, so too is the inner world of the mind.

5. Consider the toys of the child; the dramas of the teen; the adventures of the young adult; the joys and burdens of family life; the aches and pains of aging; and the death throes at the end. These widely varied experiences may seem surreal or dream-like when we look back at them through the decades.

6. No matter how varied our life's experiences are, they are strung like beads on the one singular thought of "I." Just as God the Father remains beyond and untouched by the dream world, this "I" also has a similar character of sameness, of being unchanged throughout life.

* See chapter eight: "The Meaning of Duality."

Chapter 8

The Meaning of Duality

I HAVE COME TO LEARN IN MY RESEARCH THAT THE concept of duality has several interpretations. Earlier I presented the basic concept of duality as giving rise to the illusion of matter being created by the duality of opposites: movement from a center of rest. (The movement being the vibration of the Word/Holy Ghost and the center of rest being the immanent consciousness of the Christ universal, son of God.)

Duality as expressed in *Sanatan Dharma* is not the teaching that there exists eternally and in absolute terms two opposite but equal forces such as light or dark, good or evil. Though we often speak in such terms, the opposites are limited to the creation. They are not absolute. They are only relative to the One, to the Absolute which transcends good, bad, light, and dark. Let's explore this further.

The entire cosmos ranging from our private thoughts and emotions to planets and quarks is created by the outflowing Holy Ghost vibration (or Word) of God. As discussed previously, some of the Beings commissioned to assist with the creation rebelled against the purity of intention behind the creation. It's as if the outflowing, but conscious, energy reached a point of no return where the alignment with God's intention was so stretched that those responsible for the work of creation broke away from that intention and "set up shop" for themselves. Thus, evil is the *absence* of good, matter *masks* consciousness. Evil is ignorance and forgetfulness. It pursues material ends as the goodness it desires, but from which it can never find lasting fulfillment. It is not the opposite but the *absence* of God.

Thus, there are two kinds of duality: one vertical, the other horizontal. The horizontal duality is what we usually think of when we say male vs female; light vs dark; good vs bad. In the horizontal version, the opposites are equals. They are opposite from the center of rest between them. The center of rest represents the indwelling Christ consciousness, or causal realm of the pure soul.

But the lesser-known duality is the vertical: consciousness of God being projected away from God and out into the universe. Imagine a great light. Near the source it is very bright, but as the light shines further and further out into the darkness of space it becomes dimmer until all one sees is darkness. In this duality the opposites are NOT equals but the one is the absence of the other.

Cross the two dualities and you have the symbol of the cross. The horizontal relates to the world around us, the world of the senses and matter. The vertical relates to our soul's relationship (close or distant) to God. The outflowing energy of the Holy Spirit (aka *AUM* or Divine Mother) can get to a point where it is no longer recognizable. But the strong magnetism of God, the source, creates an opposite pull, drawing the nescient and prodigal soul back to its home in God.

In the Eastern teachings we speak often of duality, but it is not always the case that opposites are equals. God, or good, prevails in the sense that the darkness, or evil at least, never wins. Mahatma Gandhi stated, "When I despair, I remember that all through history the way of truth and love has always won. There have been tyrants and murderers and for a time they seem invincible, but in the end, they always fall . . . think of it, always."

A metaphor that combines both the vertical and the horizontal can be described in the movement of a pendulum from side to side. The top part of the pendulum moves far less side to side than the bottom. While all objects and thoughts are in motion, some — those nearer the top — are calm and never stray far from the center. In the pendulum metaphor, Christ consciousness, son of God, resides at the center point between the two opposites while God the Father beyond creation resides motionless at the top of the pendulum.

When Yogananda would describe duality by saying "Better to be good than bad because the villain in the play dies or is imprisoned," he is referring to the vertical duality. Goodness, though in one sense opposite to badness, is closer, nonetheless to the calm vibration and purity of Spirit. The Spirit is beyond duality.

In our personal day-to-day lives, and on the stage of history from century-to-century, the opposites vie for attention and prominence. In their outward appearance, at the bottom of the pendulum, they may seem equal, but they are not because the very pendulum descends from Spirit and goodness is higher up the pendulum, closer to God.* Nonetheless,

* The motivation for goodness can be low (wanting approval) to high (an unseen act of devotion) or as a channel of soul-guidance.

virtue is not the same as Self-realization. It exists in the horizontal duality of creation. It is not absolute, but it is a step in that direction because its origin is nearer the top of the pendulum. So long as the ego views its virtue as the result of its own actions, being the Doer of actions, virtue cannot free us from either action or duality. We can aspire to goodness in one department of our life but find we are not so good in another. We cannot achieve the perfection to which Christ called us by virtue alone. Grace holds the key to perfecting our efforts. Souls have an infinity of time and incarnations to awaken to the benefits of goodness, and from there to awaken to seek the Source of goodness.

Yet, as they evidently said in the Middle Ages, "The road to hell is paved with good intentions."* Virtue, in the human sense, is not powerful enough to lead by itself to freedom in God. Soul freedom is achieved only by the conscious act of seeking God. Virtue may be its own reward, as the cliché asserts, but in the *Sanatan Dharma* view it is merely "good karma" and the karma bank of virtue will get drawn upon by the inexorable movement of that pendulum from side to side. The individual soul, not a nation or a family, must "make love to God."† Like Job in the Old Testament, the righteous person will be tested. If his righteousness is not of God, if it is attached to the good and prosperous fruit of virtue, he will curse the Maker for his woes.

The opposites in their outer appearance may seem equal, but the "dice are loaded" because the horizontal duality descends from the One behind all appearances.

* This saying has been attributed to Bernard of Clairvaux (1091–1153) but this cannot be verified. It appeared in a newspaper in 1833 and in a different form in 1670 in a Collection of English Proverbs by John Ray.
† A phrase Yogananda sometimes used.

PART TWO

Salvation

Chapter 9

The Word Was Made Flesh

THE TEACHING OF *SANATAN DHARMA* SAYS THAT THE son of God dwells in all souls as the Christ consciousness. It stands to reason that there must be some souls who have "realized" this fact. It would also be reasonable to imagine that at least some of them would either stick around or come back later to tell the rest of us "the good news." Indeed, that is the teaching of the East. In India there is a Sanskrit word for such a soul: an *avatar*. Jesus Christ is considered an *avatar* by most Hindus. So are Rama, Krishna, Buddha, and many others. Some also consider Paramhansa Yogananda and his lineage to be *avatars* for the modern age.

Genesis says God made us in His image. And God declared to Moses "I AM THAT I AM."* So also, the Indian scriptures proclaim in Sanskrit: "*Tat Twam Asi*"† — Thou art that.

But unless divinity takes human form, how can we dare to affirm that we, too, are *that*? Thousands listened to Jesus Christ preach his parables, but few followed him. "It takes

---

* Exodus 3:14–15
† Chandogya Upanishad, Chapter 6

one to know one" we used to taunt back on the school playground when we were called names.

I never tire of telling the story and feeling the divine power that must have been exchanged between Jesus and Peter when Peter responded to Jesus' question, "Who do men say I am?" Peter, and only Peter, looking as I imagine he did into the eyes of Jesus, spoke the immortal words from a higher state of consciousness "Thou art the Christ, the son of the living God."[*]

The "rock" upon which Jesus said he'd build "my church" was, Yogananda stated, the bedrock of intuitive knowing that "flesh and blood" (reason and the senses) could not reveal.[†] It is intuition, which Yogananda defined as "The soul's power to know God," that gives the keys to the kingdom of God within you. Spirit is "super-natural" and natural living (meaning reason and common sense) cannot reveal the existence of the soul (or God).[‡]

Just One Christ?

There is no devotion greater or more important to a true Christian than that offered to Jesus Christ. The testimony of the greatest saints of Christianity affirms the life, teachings, and the omnipresent existence of Jesus Christ. Is it possible, therefore, for Christianity to admit into its worldview the existence of other Christs? It doesn't seem so for now, but I think it *will* come. The continuing and growing contact with other faith traditions, commingled together throughout the

---

[*] Matt 16:16

[†] I believe this is the only instance of Jesus being quoted as referring to a church, what to mention "my church." The words of scripture often contain several levels of meaning, each of which contains some truth.

[‡] In Sankhya teachings of India, it says "Iswar-ashidha" — God cannot be proved (by reason).

world in every city and town, must surely prod Christians to think more broadly. As Christians learn about the saints of other faiths it becomes increasingly difficult to deny the omnipresent living Christ, the "Word made flesh," residing in other souls. It cannot fail to happen for the simple reason that it is true.

Our world is closing in upon us. Separation and sectarianism are increasingly unnatural, unhealthy, and awkward. Life is crying out for acceptance and understanding of the underlying and uniting truth of the One God. We see this impulse expressed in science in its efforts to discover the underlying and universal laws of nature. Sadly, I know that there are some orthodox religionists who cling stubbornly to the unique and exclusive claims of their respective dogmas.

The outer forms of dogmas, customs, traditions, and rituals of the different faith traditions need not be discarded for they can be beautiful, meaningful, and inspiring. But at this point in history, admission by the different orthodox faiths that other faiths may be of equal spiritual value is far from forthcoming. Acceptance of other religions is the first step; then comes respect, but respect is not the same as the recognition of equality, though it is a step in the right direction.

Swami Kriyananda was in Thailand many years ago and found a pamphlet at a Buddhist shrine saying, in effect, "Yes, all religions are good but to achieve nirvana one must first reincarnate as a Buddhist." I dimly recall Christians or perhaps Catholics (since I was raised Catholic) talking about so-called "natural" religions. Somehow people in such religions might still have a chance for heaven provided they didn't hear about or did not reject Christianity.*

---

* Golly, I say, that's awfully "big" of them.

Would the possibility of other Christ-like saviors diminish the spiritual power and stature of Jesus Christ? Admittedly, it would undermine the *exclusive* claims of Christians, but it need not diminish the stature of Jesus Christ as a son of God. As Yogananda put it, "One who knows God, is God."*

In the first chapter of the Gospel of John we read "and as many as received Him to them gave He the power to become the sons of God." When accused of blasphemy for announcing that "I and my Father are One" Jesus retorted, quoting the Old Testament, "Do not your scriptures say, 'Ye are gods?'"†

Paramhansa Yogananda often cited these two quotes from the Bible noted above. Another quote he used is Jesus' statement to the effect that "the things I do ye shall do and greater things than these."‡ Of course, this by itself doesn't necessitate the implication that the apostles had achieved the Self-realized stature of Jesus, but it is suggestive of their potential, and by extension, ours as well.

At the Last Supper, Jesus washes the feet of the disciples showing how they were to serve one another and others. He declares that from then on, they are "friends" and not servants of their Master.§ In Jesus' prayer to the Father as reported by John in Chapter 17 of his gospel, he states "I pray . . . that they [his disciples] all may be one; as thou, Father, art in me, and I in thee, that they also may be one in us; . . . that they may be

---

* He also cautioned that such a one should not say, "I am God." Rather, "God has become me." Or, as Jesus put it "I and my Father are One." A soul who achieves Self-realization is not greater nor lesser than any other who has achieved final emancipation from delusion even if their roles in this world may be greater or lesser.

† Psalms 82:6; John 10:34

‡ John 14:12

§ John 15:14–15

one, even as we are one. . . . I in them, and thou in me, that they may be made perfect in one. . . ."*

Jesus said, "Before Abraham was, I AM!"† So, let's see, Jesus existed before the beginning of the world as what? A human? In a human body? Hmmm. . . . I don't think that's what he meant. The son of God, who according to the Gospel of John, was the Word, was with God in the beginning, made all things, and was the life of and light of men, was obviously not a human person. St. John does not even mention Jesus' name until the end of the first chapter. "The Word became flesh"‡ but how could one human incarnation limit the Word in any way? The "Word" would remain eternal and omnipresent.

Devotees of Lord Krishna, like their Christian counterparts, believe their Lord is the direct incarnation of God in human form. One of the early challenges to the new Christian faith was the Arian heresy wherein it was held that the nature of Jesus was "begotten of the Father," meaning a being created by God and therefore not one with the Father. Some versions of this insisted that Jesus therefore was human, not divine. One of the unforgivable tenants of some of the Gnostics was that Jesus did not suffer on the cross because he *was* God. Was Jesus man or God? This controversy culminated in the dogma of the Holy Trinity: three in one. Suffice to say, the question of "Who am I" has been at the core of the Christian faith and mystery. Perhaps our understanding is finally ready to evolve to the next, deeper and more universal level. Put another way, this question is the existential challenge that confronts each one of us, not just Jesus Christ.

* John 17:20–22
† John 8:58
‡ John 1:14

The teachings of *Sanatan Dharma* and Paramhansa Yogananda specifically say that in all cases, whether Krishna, Jesus, Buddha, and other saints, they are souls like you and me, but they are souls who have achieved Self-realization. They have become "one with the Father." In truth, God is the *only* reality and our purpose in life is to realize this as our own true Self. Thus, Yogananda offers what seems an acceptable basis for expanding the son of Godship without diminishing Jesus or Krishna or anyone else. As taught since ancient times, the key is found in the Sanskrit expression, *Tat Twam Asi*: "Thou art that."* What these souls who return as saviors (*avatars*) have that is distinct from you and me is that they have achieved and reclaimed their divine birthright. They do not differ from us in kind but in degree only.

The entire creation is God, though admittedly well disguised. Most objects in the creation are not sufficiently self-aware to achieve Self-realization. The human-divine nature of Jesus presents the same paradox for him as it does for us. Our souls are sparks of the Infinite Being. As such we too have existed for eternity. We too are "as old as God." We too can say "Before Abraham was, I AM." But the ego cannot say this; only the soul can come to this realization within itself.

In past lives an *avatar* is one who has achieved liberation from the delusion of separateness and has thus achieved the power to defy death itself: to raise the dead, to resurrect our mortal remains, to heal the blind and the lame, to forgive sins, and to cast out demons. More importantly than these powers, which even lesser saints (not fully God-realized) have demonstrated, is the power to transmit the state of God-realization to another soul.

* See also Genesis 1:26–27 Man is made in the image of God.

Most saints are almost but not completely "there." They may uplift a few disciples but do not have the lasting power that can stand the test of centuries. Some disciples of Jesus (or Krishna, etc.) have achieved their spiritual freedom even centuries after the human life of their savior. That such savior-*avatars* would have the power to free other souls centuries later suggests to us a valid reason why they are called "world saviors."

Is there a top dog among them? Yogananda said that once the soul has achieved permanent union with God it cannot "fall" spiritually. All souls who have achieved God-realization are equal, he added. Freedom from sin, ignorance or delusion is assured eternally. Some may have a dramatic outward role in history such as Jesus did. Others may serve unknown to the world at large. Mahavatar Babaji, featured in Yogananda's autobiography, is described as one who works behind the human stage of history to guide prophets in directing the spiritual upliftment of the epoch in which we live. He is, one could say, a prophet's prophet. But he works mostly in anonymity, except to a handful of disciples. He is not greater than other *avatars*, but he has a unique role.

The role that an *avatar* plays in this world isn't something they choose, for no ego remains. To reincarnate into human form, even an *avatar* needs a body and therefore needs the function of the ego to "keep it together," but the *avatar* is not forced to reincarnate by the burden of past karma.

This concept of the universal Christ state-of-consciousness being fully realized by an individual soul thus reconciles the innate divinity of the creation with the appearance of this consciousness in human form. The Christ consciousness is at the heart of everything but functions unrealized; unrecognized. ("Who do men say I AM?")

Only in the human form does it have the potential (and destiny) to achieve the fullness of humanity and the fullness of divinity at the same time and in the same form. In India, this state is called by many names such as *moksha*, but is also the state of yoga, or union.*

In this view Jesus suffers no diminution of status and joins in fellowship with the lineage of *avatars* who in every age are "the Word made flesh" and who dwell among us.

I said earlier that the Word is the vibratory creation which can be seen, and the Christ consciousness is the invisible intelligence which inhabits the Word. The analogy is the difference between our mind and our body. When the Christ consciousness takes human form the two are becoming one and those two are, at the same time, "one with the Father."

Is There a Relationship Between Jesus Christ and Any Other Avatar?

This question is a side topic. It is not central to my purpose, but it is often asked. Yogananda, when asked "Why do you place special emphasis on the teachings of Jesus and those of Krishna," responded saying "It was Babaji's wish that I do so." At that moment he must have felt not to say more. But in his life, teachings, and writings he gave hints.

Perhaps the most obvious hint is his public statement that the three Wise Men were none other than the guru-preceptors of his own lineage: Babaji, Lahiri Mahasaya, and Swami Sri Yukteswar. If so, then who does that make Jesus? He never said, so far as I know.

* The term "yoga" is related etymologically to our word "yoke." The word "religion" comes from the Latin, "religare," to bind.

Yogananda also enthusiastically endorsed the story told by Nicolas Notovitch in a book titled *The Unknown Life of Jesus Christ*. This book describes the "lost" eighteen years of Jesus' early life. Jesus was reported to have gone to India and Tibet. It is curious that if this had been so, why did the gospels omit any reference to Jesus' whereabouts for these important years? At least they didn't have the audacity to insert some other narrative. Truthfulness presumably precluded making up a story, but discretion and fear of its implications perhaps encouraged them to "drop the subject."*

So far as I know, Yogananda did not comment on other stories such as the assertion that Jesus survived the crucifixion and ended up in Kashmir (or elsewhere). Yogananda endorsed the narrative of the crucifixion and resurrection of Jesus Christ.

On a more personal note, when I first read Yogananda's autobiography I intuitively felt, without considering consciously its implications, that Yogananda was a reincarnation of Jesus Christ. I think I can safely say that Swami Kriyananda did, or probably did, but he, too, was circumspect. When in my early years I made the comment to Swami Kriyananda, "Of course, Yogananda *couldn't* have been Jesus in a past life because he, himself, writes of having more than one vision of Jesus Christ!" Swamiji's response was "Why not?"

In his public talks, Swami Kriyananda would sometimes state that from the eternal now and infinity of Spirit, any person who lived at any time in the past, and especially a

* I ask myself: would I have dropped the subject if I had been in their place? Imagine how confusing it would have been to preach the gospel throughout the Roman Empire while including in the narrative Jesus' journey and training in India. The result would be that thousands would have rushed off to India. This was destined to be delayed until the nineteenth and twentieth centuries.

great saint, can be "called out" of the Spirit by the devotion of another soul even if that saint was now incarnated into a new form and new life. I believe that is what Swami Kriyananda meant when he said, "Why not?"

As I said, this topic is not of central concern to this book or to Yogananda's purpose of showing the underlying similarities between Christianity and what he sometimes called "Hindu Yoga." Typically, Yogananda used words like "underlying similarities between the teachings of Jesus Christ and those of Lord Krishna." By "Hindu Yoga" he meant the core teachings of *Sanatan Dharma* which predate the appearance of Hinduism in its present and cultural form.

There is, however, a connection between Yogananda and Jesus Christ and between the core teachings of India and Christianity.

One theory I have for this connection is that both Indian spiritual teachings and Christianity contain the clearest expression of the concept that God takes human form for the salvation of souls. The teaching of the role and need for the savior-guru appears in its clearest form in Indian teachings and in Christianity, though in Christianity it is not a principle, for it is limited to the person of Jesus Christ.

Chapter 10

The Soul's Need for a Guru

IT IS TAUGHT IN *SANATAN DHARMA* THAT THE SOUL achieves salvation (called *moksha* in Sanskrit) through a divinely ordained guru. If you reread the Last Supper, Jesus makes it clear that the disciples were given to him by God for their salvation.* It was *not* a choice they made, though when Jesus said to each, "Come follow me," they always had a choice. The teaching both in Christianity and in *Sanatan Dharma* is that the agent of our salvation is known from the beginning of time. Our path to that One is determined by the many choices that we make over many lifetimes. But eventually when our soul, like the prodigal son, turns home to God, the depth of our sincere effort magnetically draws to us that soul who is "our own."† We might go through many stages and even many teachers (including over lifetimes, different faith traditions) but in the last stages of our salvation the "sat guru" (the true guru) comes to redeem us. This teaching is a beautiful promise and an expression of the unconditional love of

* John 17:6
† This is a loose analogy to how we find our marriage partner, which is something more common to the human experience.

God for each soul. It is the promise that God takes human form to free us from the prison of our ego.

The sat guru can come through disciples of the guru but at some point, before the "end," we will meet our sat guru. A savior is not barred by distance or time for such a soul has achieved omnipresence and omniscience in the Spirit of the Father and is truly a "son of God."

There are many aspects to the teaching of the soul's need for a guru. It would be beyond the scope of this book to present a complete "case" for it. I refer you to the summary of Yogananda's teachings as compiled by Swami Kriyananda in the book *The Essence of Self-Realization*. But a few comments on this teaching are appropriate partly because in Christianity this teaching isn't codified as a principle because Jesus is "the only one." But in *Sanatan Dharma* the teaching finds frequent and universal expression.

If we could achieve cosmic consciousness, or union with God, by our own willpower we would be strengthening the very vortex of ego that prevents us from knowing God and which must be discarded to achieve Oneness. Our salvation therefore faces a fundamental conundrum. How can the "I" of ego, having separated itself from God countless eons ago, reunite with God by self-effort alone?

The need for the power of God through the guru to complete the journey of Self-realization (redemption) is the reason such saviors as Jesus, Krishna, and others declare that "I am the way, the truth and the light." It is also the truth behind the saying that by "works we are not saved, but by grace."*

You might ask why the indwelling Christ consciousness is not sufficient for the soul's redemption and why the Christ

* Ephesians 2:8–10

must take human form to achieve it? Here the Christian teaching of original sin meets the teaching of karma and re-incarnation in *Sanatan Dharma*. Our past actions are not so summarily dismissed by our good intentions. For one thing, the threads of past actions in previous incarnations and their concomitant consequences are hidden from us. They consti-tute an inner labyrinth through which orderly and efficient escape is all but impossible with the limited tools of the in-tellect, willpower and ego.

Working step by step on our personal imperfections is to use a simile that Swami Kriyananda employed, like washing a shirt in a bucket: no sooner do you hold one part under water than another part pops up. As he once discovered as a young monk, "I worked so diligently on developing devotion that I discovered I was proud of my humility."

There is a story that Swami Kriyananda heard from Yogananda and often told: A man was being harassed by a demon. He learned a mantra from a rishi and the next time the demon appeared the man chanted the mantra over a pow-der which he threw onto the demon (as he had been instruct-ed to do). The demon, however, laughed and said, "Before you could say your mantra I entered into the powder!" The ego infects our very aspiration to transcend it. An outside force, the guru's grace, is needed to defeat the demon-ego.

The built-in limits of the power of self-will are illustrated in the story of Moses. Though he was the one who led the chil-dren of Israel from captivity, he could not enter the Promised Land. Yogananda explained that Moses symbolizes the ego and though he was a true master, it was for illustrating this principle that the story prevents Moses from entering. The ego can lead our tendencies (children), but only so far.

Similarly in the Indian epic of the *Mahabharata*, the grandsire Bhishma symbolizes ego. In that story's great war, Bhishma had the boon to decide when to die, illustrating that it is the ego alone that must surrender to God as the indwelling soul.

The sacrifice that the saviors of humanity make is to retake human form. Though in their souls they are one with God, the human form contains inherent limitations compared to cosmic consciousness. Along with the usual lessons that an infant, toddler, teen, and adult must contend with in human form, the *avatar* must contend with the indifference and persecution it endures from humanity. We, however aspiring and desirous to know God, are stuck in human form, a vicious cycle as it were. To start the engine of our soul's power, a booster from an outside source is needed.

However, rather than condemn the human form as a delusion, human life was intended to be experienced in God consciousness. This is the lesson behind the existence of the Garden of Eden. There are similar so-called creation myths that paint a similar picture of harmony in the long-forgotten past with the Creator. Besides, what would be the purpose of saying we are made in the image of God and are children of God if human existence must be obliterated in order to achieve union with God, our Creator? Stories from India imply that angels and other such exalted beings desire human existence for they know that such is a steppingstone to God realization which is withheld from them.

God doesn't want the creation to be rejected as evil. The great game of "hide and seek" that God plays through the mask of creation can only achieve its purpose when God discovers God behind the appearances of form. The *sat guru* (true guru or savior) is the living proof that Self-realization can be achieved in human form. Indeed, even the angels and higher beings are said to not yet possess this achievement, for it can only be won in the human form.

And finally, we must work out and release our past attachments (*karma*) to the creation before we can earn permanent and eternal repose in the Spirit. Until we do, we are required by the burden of our karma to return to this school of life.

Chapter 11

How Does God View Suffering?

S OME SAY THAT FROM THE GOD'S-EYE PERSPECTIVE
good and evil have their place. This is surely true
from the holodeck of Infinity.* But if God is immanent in all things, then God is both large and small; infinite
and infinitesimal; impersonal and personal (as in you and
me). God does not want us to suffer but the rules of the
game of creation are such that God must also play by the
rules. Yet, as I wrote above, the dice are loaded (with God
being in them already).† Suffering, you see, is what triggers
the human mind to ask hard questions. If life were easy, we
would probably never seek the meaning of it. "An easy life
is not a victorious life," Yogananda would say. He quoted
God in the form of his beloved Divine Mother as saying,
"To those to whom I give much (in money, fame etc.), I do
not give myself." Jesus said something about how difficult
it is for a rich person to enter the kingdom of heaven.‡

---

* The "holodeck" is a fictional device from the television franchise *Star Trek*
which, among other uses, could allow a space traveler to go on a "vacation" to
their favorite place. It used holograms to create the appearance of reality.

† Like, but opposite of, the story of the demon quoted earlier.

‡ Matt 19:24

Even suffering is "loaded" and used for good, by God, to prod the soul back toward goodness, virtue, and, eventually, to seeking God alone above all else. Without suffering, we would never seek to befriend "the man behind the curtain."* Thus, suffering is a necessary ingredient to the soul's journey from "foreign lands" back to our home in God.

Think how much of human culture, arts, history, and relationships are focused on war, genocide, exploitation, and abuse.† No one writes an engaging novel about a pleasant church picnic. Our mettle is tested, and we are potentially ennobled by our tests and trials. Many days we may wish it were not so but the "pearl of great price" or the Holy Grail of God's bliss is not won cheaply.

Yogananda said that sometimes he would argue with the Divine Mother, scolding her for having created us and our problems, with the consequence of so much human suffering. He said God accepts this scolding, and why not? We didn't create ourselves or this world. Moreover, the power of delusion and addiction are stronger and greater than any one person. Anger, hatred, lust, avarice, etc.: these are all vibrations of consciousness that preexist the fact of our being tempted by them. Drugs, alcohol, unrestrained sex, violence: such things have a magnetism greater than our own. Fortunately, so does goodness, kindness, compassion, and self-sacrifice. We sit in between them with an angel on our right and the devil on our left. Yogananda is famously quoted saying "Thoughts are universally not individually rooted."

* From the movie *The Wizard of Oz* when the wizard is discovered to be only a man.
† The beloved scripture of India, the Bhagavad Gita, takes place on a real battlefield: though a historically true event, the scripture itself is a metaphor for the battle of the soul for victory.

But the good news is embedded in the bad news: if the magnetism of evil is greater than our own personal magnetism, so too is the power that created us greater than our own power. It is by grace that we are uplifted, not by our power alone.* Our choice is to attune ourselves to one or the other. The power of one, or the other, will join with ours and move us along in the chosen direction. As pointed out earlier, it's not as if they are equal in power because delusion contains within it the seeds of our awakening. When we know that it is by God's power that we ascend then that power will never let us down. Krishna says to the devotee in the Bhagavad Gita "I will make good your deficiencies and render permanent your gains!"†

---

* Yogananda stated that our soul's victory is achieved by the formula of 25% our effort; 25% the effort of the guru on our behalf; and 50% the grace of God. (Of course, our effort is 100% of our will even as it is "all" God's grace for there is nothing real and eternal BUT God!)

† Bhagavad Gita 9:22

Chapter 12

Who Is the Doer of All Actions?

I F THIS WORLD IS BUT A DREAM OF GOD, THEN IT MUST BE said that God plays all the parts, whether we know it or not. When we awaken and begin cooperating with divine grace, we see all things as the hand of the loving God. We may even rightly ascribe our shortcomings to God. Yogananda said God likes it when we "blame" God for our faults. Not, of course, by way of allowing ourselves to repeat them with heedless abandon, but so that we don't identify with our "sins." "The greatest sin," he said, "is to call yourself a sinner."

There are many steps to the full realization that God is the Doer. It would help to start by simply conducting one's life and actions in alignment with our conscience and with the basic tenets of right attitude and behavior. Our conscience, as it develops and becomes increasingly refined, is the voice of the Christ consciousness within us. The good and wholesome virtues of life are there to help us understand the calming, satisfying reward of goodness. Goodness can refine our character to the point where we offer all our thoughts and actions to the Christ consciousness within. In time, and with practice, we experience an increasing flow of grace. By degrees, we become Christ-like. We "put on the Lord Jesus Christ" as St. Paul put it.*

In the teachings of yoga, this process is called *nishkam karma*: action without desire for the fruit (results) of action. We attempt to act only in accordance with duty as we can best perceive it, and without regard to personal self-interest. To this we add the presentation of the action as an act of love and devotion to God.† Next, we seek to become an instrument of the divine will: "Thy will, not my will."‡ In time both the instrument and the act are manifestations of divine energy and intelligence. God becomes the Doer of all actions in the soul of a Self-realized being.

Swami Kriyananda, in the later stages of life, commented that he no longer knew where in his consciousness he ended and where Yogananda began. Great saints of East and West attest to the increasing awareness that, as John the Baptist put it, "He (Jesus) must increase, and I must decrease."§ Saints are depicted with a halo, the nimbus, because they are often seen to radiate an inner light.

Yogananda stated "I killed Yogananda long ago. No one dwells within but God." And as Jesus put it, "I and my Father are One."¶

---

* Romans 13:14
† Krishna famously tells his disciple, Arjuna, "Even a leaf I accept if offered with devotion." Bhagavad Gita 9:26
‡ Matt 26:39
§ John 3:30
¶ John 10:30

Chapter 13

Holy Communion and Saints

I T IS THE SAINTS WHO ARE THE TRUE CUSTODIANS OF religion and truth. The personal testimony of the greatest disciples of Jesus Christ reveals the growing presence of Christ in their lives. When, at the Last Supper, Jesus gave the sacrament of bread and wine, he was saying, in effect, "take my consciousness into yourself and become a Christ."

Yogananda explained Jesus' words and action with the bread and wine in very "yogic" terms. He said the "bread" represents the universal Christ consciousness hidden invisibly in all matter. It is this "bread" that gives us life. Life is intelligence and self-awareness; a clear and active conscience; access to wisdom and innate omnipresent joy of life. The "wine" is the flowing, vibrating, vital energy underlying the diverse forms of life from which those forms appear. The former is invisible but immanent; the latter is the Holy Ghost (the *AUM* vibration) moving and producing and having the power to manifest matter and accomplishments. We have both the Christ consciousness and the Holy Ghost or Word referenced here. Jesus, the *avatar*, was both the Christ and the Word made flesh, and at the same time, "One with the Father." The mystery of the Trinity is coexistent in the God-realized soul.

To the devotee seeking God, communion is not limited to a ritual; it is *inner* communion with the Word and with the Christ-consciousness. The sacrament is an outer symbol and ritual which, imbued with the devotion and attunement of the devotee, whether priest or parishioner, can uplift the soul into true communion. Padre Pio would take three hours to perform the mass because he would become immersed in Christ-consciousness, but most priests can finish it off in twenty minutes. St. Joseph of Cupertino would levitate during the mass. Were these ecstatic experiences the result of the ritual performance of the Eucharist (the Mass) or were they the result of the devotion and attunement of these two saints?* Over two thousand years, thousands of masses have been conducted, but how many, whether priest or parishioner, have entered such a state of ecstasy?

It is foolish to imagine the Eucharist is the only ritual on the planet during which saintly souls have entered the holy state of inner communion. If the sacrament of the Eucharist can elevate your soul into what Yogananda called "super-consciousness" then go for it. But Yogananda reintroduced meditation to the West because in stillness and silence (not merely in outward prayers, standing, kneeling, and moving around) God can be most readily perceived. "Be still and know. . . ."† Did not Jesus himself counsel us to "go into our closet" to pray?‡

* I suppose the orthodox explanation says these spiritual experiences are the result solely of grace. This at least deflects some attention from the saint so that other priests can save face but, let's face it, the grace flows from the effort towards sanctity expressed by the saint. Once again, the mantra "Both-And" comes in handy.
† Psalm 46:10
‡ "But thou, when thou prayest, enter into thy closet, and when thou hast shut thy door, pray to thy Father which is in secret; and thy Father which seeth in secret shall reward thee openly." Matt 6:6

Chapter 14

Self-Realization

WHAT IS THE NATURE OF THIS STATE OF INNER communion? What is mystical marriage, as it has been called in Christianity? Although it is the core of all true spiritual teachings, I am not going to dwell on it in this book. Why? Because that which is beyond words is, well, beyond words. My purpose, as was Yogananda's, is to show the underlying similarity in the expressed teachings of Christ (New Testament, especially) and Krishna (Bhagavad Gita).

Countless scriptures, poems, songs, and lectures have attempted to describe that state which is indescribable. Countless, too, are its names: *samadhi*, cosmic consciousness, satori, heaven, union with God, yoga, mystical marriage, enlightenment, *moksha*, freedom, salvation, and on and on. Futile would be the attempt to define such a state. Throughout this book I am referring to this state in various ways. The great Christian mystics from St. Francis to Padre Pio and the innumerable yogis, sages, shamans, and others testify it is the summum bonum of life. Yogananda's poem, "Samadhi," is a wonderful and modern description of the state as are several stories in his now famous autobiography.*

In a later chapter, however, I will attempt to share an insight given to us by Paramhansa Yogananda on the ego's expansion into divine union.

---

* See *Autobiography of a Yogi*, for both the poem and the stories. Read for free: https://www.ananda.org/autobiography/

Chapter 15

Did Jesus Die for Our Sins?

W HAT DOES IT MEAN WHEN CHRISTIANS SAY THAT "Jesus died for our sins?"

It seems a bit of a stretch to say that Jesus' death on the cross forgives the sins of all those who "believe on his name."* That's a lot of sins committed in two thousand plus years.† There's no point trying to convince anyone, but I can only ascribe such a statement to pious sentiment. Yet, as in so many beliefs, there is a measure of truth. Let's explore wherein lies the seed of truth.

Before I continue, I'd like to add a bit of esoterica here: the "name" of God isn't an ordinary word in English or any other language.‡ The "name" of God, it is taught in

---

* John 1:12

† Forgiveness in exchange for three hours on the cross, and all night before, being interrogated, whipped, and humiliated. Torture for sure, but how does one weigh its value? How does one weigh the depth of a Christian's conversion, belief, and life transformation? How many Christians demonstrate in their lives that they have been "saved"?

‡ Even though a person's name can be spelled out in letters, one can have a name even if one's language has no script. A name is a sound, as is any word. A sound is spoken and heard through the medium of vibration: first in the thought or intention to speak the name, and then in its utterance. God's name is the sound of God's consciousness manifesting creation through the progressive stages of thought, energy and matter.

Sanatan Dharma, is the vibration of the *AUM* or Amen: a vibration heard intuitively, usually in a deep state of prayer and meditation. Those who "believe on his name" would include those who seek inner communion with the vibratory presence of God within. Inner communion with *AUM* is an aspect or a description of true baptism since Yogananda taught that *AUM is* the Holy Spirit.

I can accept that for the encouragement of church goers or new initiates, it is helpful to state that even believers have a chance to become the sons of God. Not, however, for merely believing, but for the fact that belief is the natural starting point in the journey towards realization.

Jesus stated at various times and in various ways "I am the way, the truth, and the life: no man cometh unto the Father but by me."* This is a strong statement. Christians relate the personal pronoun "I" to the person of Jesus Christ. I have written repeatedly that in the teachings of *Sanatan Dharma* this "I" is the universal consciousness immanent in all creation. But either way, what are its implications?

There are two metaphysical principles suggested here: the forgiveness of sins by a savior (*avatar*) in respect to the karma (sins) of a disciple; and the role of the savior (*avatar*) in the salvation of the soul.

What is the consequence of having one's sins forgiven? Shouldn't there be tangible evidence of forgiveness? The penitent should be cleansed from repeating the sin; or at least, be deeply repentant even if not yet wholly cleansed from a repeat of the transgression.

When Jesus said to the paralyzed man who was lowered

* John 14:6

through a hole in the roof of the house at which he was speaking "Your sins are forgiven," he then told the man to get up. Jesus healed the man of his physical paralysis to demonstrate that he had the power to forgive the man's sins. The physical healing was the tangible proof of his forgiveness. From the verbal exchange there's no evidence that the man sought forgiveness, only healing. Yet Jesus did both. In so doing he also inferred a nexus between the physical paralysis and past transgression.

The twentieth century stigmatist Padre Pio heard the confessions of thousands. The reports of healing through Padre Pio's intercession are countless. But if a Catholic goes to confession to their parish priest, what is forgiveness in such a case? For one thing, most supplicants probably sin again (and again); for another, I doubt the consequences of their past sinful acts are erased (at least there's little record of such things considering the millions who have given their confession). Nonetheless, according to church doctrine the penitent is absolved and now eligible to enter heaven. Is there any proof of that?

In the New Testament story of the paralyzed man cited above, Jesus told the man "Your sins are forgiven," *before* he said, "Get up and walk." Between these two statements, Jesus felt the critique of Pharisees who observed the scene and thus he said aloud "Which is easier: to say, 'Your sins are forgiven,' or to say, 'Get up and walk'? 'But so that you may know that the Son of Man has authority on the earth to forgive sins'" Jesus said to the man, "I tell you, get up, pick up your mat, and go home."* The healing thus bore evidence of Jesus' power to forgive. Do ordinary priests demonstrate this power?

---

* Luke 5:23

The power to forgive sins must surely derive from a combination of the divine attunement of the priest, and the faith
and sincerity of the penitent. Illustrative is the story of the
woman who was healed when she touched the hem of Jesus'
cloak. Jesus felt "power is gone out of me" even though other
people thronged all around him who were also seeking to
be healed. There is no indication that others in the crowd
around Jesus were healed at the same time. When the woman
admitted it was her, Jesus said "thy faith hath made thee
whole; go in peace."* I would aver that this woman's life, not
just her "hemorrhage," was changed for the better.†

The Power of a Saint to Take on the Sins of Another onto His Body

That a spiritually enlightened soul can take away the consequences of past karma from another person is a firm teaching in *Sanatan Dharma*. Yogananda's autobiography contains
several references to this.

This passage taken from *Autobiography of a Yogi* may be
helpful:

> Fortunately for his disciples, Sri Yukteswar burned many
> of their sins in the fire of his severe fever in Kashmir.
> The metaphysical method of physical transfer of disease

---

* Luke 8:43–48

† It is curious that in the Old Testament (see especially Leviticus), that animal
sacrifices and food offerings to the Lord are mandated, including for the forgiveness of sins, not just ritual offenses. I assume that the attitude of repentance was
required but I assume in such times this was one way to pay off one's karma, or,
in their words, to atone for one's transgressions. Bad karma can be offset by good
karma. The fact that wealthy industrialists inevitably become philanthropists,
suggests as much. The sale of indulgences by the Catholic Church was a blatant
fundraiser but I believe the practice continues to this day. Perhaps good deeds
can outweigh bad deeds, but "salvation" takes more than this.

is known to highly advanced yogis. A strong man can assist a weaker one by helping to carry his heavy load; a spiritual superman is able to minimize his disciples' physical or mental burdens by sharing the karma of their past actions. Just as a rich man loses some money when he pays off a large debt for his prodigal son, who is thus saved from dire consequences of his own folly, so a master willingly sacrifices a portion of his bodily wealth to lighten the misery of disciples.*

By a secret method, the yogi unites his mind and astral vehicle with those of a suffering individual; the disease is conveyed, wholly or in part, to the saint's body. Having harvested God on the physical field, a master no longer cares what happens to that material form. Though he may allow it to register a certain disease in order to relieve others, his mind is never affected; he considers himself fortunate in being able to render such aid.

The devotee who has achieved final salvation in the Lord finds that his body has completely fulfilled its purpose; he can then use it in any way he deems fit. His work in the world is to alleviate the sorrows of mankind, whether through spiritual means or by intellectual counsel or through willpower or by the physical transfer of disease. Escaping to the super-consciousness whenever he so desires, a master can remain oblivious of physical suffering; sometimes he chooses to bear bodily pain stoically, as an example

---

* Many Christian saints, including Therese Neumann, are familiar with the metaphysical transfer of disease.

to disciples. By putting on the ailments of others, a yogi can satisfy, for them, the karmic law of cause and effect. This law is mechanically or mathematically operative; its workings can be scientifically manipulated by men of divine wisdom.

The spiritual law does not require a master to become ill whenever he heals another person. Healings ordinarily take place through the saint's knowledge of various methods of instantaneous cure in which no hurt to the spiritual healer is involved. On rare occasions, however, a master who wishes to greatly quicken his disciples' evolution may then voluntarily work out on his own body a large measure of their undesirable karma.

Jesus signified himself as a ransom for the sins of many. With his divine powers,* his body could never have been subjected to death by crucifixion if he had not willingly cooperated with the subtle cosmic law of cause and effect. He thus took on himself the consequences of others' karma, especially that of his disciples. In this manner they were highly purified and made fit to receive the omnipresent consciousness which later descended on them.

Although we don't know the "mechanics" of how an *avatar* can forgive sins (take away the karma), think of how many devices and processes we employ in daily life that we

---

* Jesus said, just before he was led away to be crucified: "Thinkest thou that I cannot now pray to my Father, and he shall presently give me more than twelve legions of angels? But how then shall the scriptures be fulfilled, that thus it must be?" Matt 26:53–54.

do not understand. The proof of forgiveness of sins must be in the changes wrought in the penitent's life. In the case of those who went to Padre Pio, countless are the numbers who changed their way of life and turned toward God.

We Don't Know What We Don't Know

As I wrote earlier, we cannot easily appreciate how deeply steeped in materialistic thinking our culture has become. We have arrived at this state in no small measure because of the burden of superstition, unproven dogmas, and unrighteousness expressed by religionists of prior centuries. We have a long way to go in terms of mass consciousness but for those with "ears to hear" and hearts open to higher realities, God is always here and now, timeless, and timely. In the chapter of his autobiography called "The Law of Miracles," Yogananda wrote:

> From science, then, if it must be so, let man learn the philosophic truth that there is no material universe; its warp and woof is *maya*, illusion. Its mirages of reality all break down under analysis. As one by one the reassuring props of a physical cosmos crash beneath him, man dimly perceives his idolatrous reliance, his past transgression of the divine command: "Thou shalt have no other gods before Me."

Grace Responds to Our Effort

If the son of a rich man gets himself into debt as a result of foolish behavior his father has the power to pay off that debt. But a wise parent might not make this choice if the child does not repent. A stronger person helping a weaker person is a common experience (and a good thing). If we are willing to sacrifice our time, talents, or resources to help others, why wouldn't the Almighty do the same for us if we are sincere in our intention to reform?

The indwelling Christ is our helpmate. Because we have been endowed with free choice, this indwelling wisdom and power will not impose itself upon us but will invite us to "look up" to "hear" the guidance of conscience and the whispers of intuition. The more we listen, the more grace will talk (that is, pour into our hearts and minds).

When the Holy Ghost came upon the apostles on Pentecost Day, surely it didn't do so except by their receptivity. We don't hear about the Holy Ghost going around "bothering" people, do we?

Sin Is Ignorance

Paramhansa Yogananda defined sin as ignorance. Even the extreme case of a person deliberately being evil is still a case of mistaken identity. If I knew that the other person was a part of myself, why would I hurt them? Humanity's original sin is the mistaken identity that we are separate from God and from all other beings and objects. Based on this error, we seek our fulfillment irrespective of the well-being of others.

Forgiveness is the act of resolving the original error of mistaken identity by reestablishing our identity with God and with others. Not surprisingly, given the profound existential implications of sin, ignorance, and the need for forgiveness, we find that forgiveness occurs frequently in the Bible. The New Testament has fifty-eight references to it, and in the entire standard Bible there are one-hundred-nine.

In the yoga teachings, the term for sin is *karma*. Karma equates to any ego-driven thought or act, whether virtuous or sinful. So long as we act in the consciousness of our separate ego we must endure the boomerang effects of karma, whether gratefully or fearfully received. In this view any act initiated by ego-driven impulses (good, bad, or indifferent) generates karma that is tied to that ego. The distinction between virtuous action and sin is only a matter of degree, for while virtuous actions are superior to evil actions, the soul is transcendent to all forms of duality (as is God). Virtue is the pathway to transcendence, but it is not, by itself, the goal.*

We are freed from our past sin or karma by the power of grace. There is no other way because a power greater than our karma, greater than ego-motivated action, is necessary to break the chains of causation. Grace, like sunshine, is always there. We need only cooperate with it, like opening the curtains of our mind and heart to let the sunshine of divine grace enter the room of our life. Effort and grace go hand in hand. The instrument of grace pouring into human lives is the human incarnation of the Christ consciousness in the form of the sat guru, the savior.

What Did Jesus Say Would Not Be Forgiven?

There is a curious statement in the gospel of Matthew that says, "blasphemy against the Holy Ghost shall not be forgiven," while whoever speaks against "the Son of man" (meaning Jesus) will be forgiven.† Yogananda explained that since the Holy Ghost represents the divinity dwelling within us, only we

---

* Since medieval times there has existed a cliché that says "The road to hell is paved with good intentions." Virtue is not enough; grace supplies the necessary power to rise spiritually. I have been told that some Christians denounce the practice of meditation in the false belief that meditation is solely an act of self-effort and does not seek or rely upon grace. Such people have obviously never tried to contact God through meditation!

† Matt 12:32

can decide to reject or accept our spiritual nature. But speaking against the guru can be forgiven since the guru appears as a human being like you and me. The guru has a face, a body, and even a personality of sorts. Even if the guru is obviously wise and loving, the guru appears (merely) human. Besides, maybe the person who speaks against the guru is destined to find some other spiritual path and guru. Consider, for example, how many thousands encountered Jesus during the three plus years of his public ministry and, by contrast, how few remained at the crucifixion. Put another way: how many cried "Hosanna" on Palm Sunday and a week later, on Good Friday, cried "Crucify him!" Few people are like Peter who could declare from intuition "Thou art the Christ." And yet even Peter, you may recall, denied being a follower of Jesus on that dreadful night that Jesus was betrayed in the garden of Gethsemane.

Years, decades, and indeed centuries after the life of such a one, it is far easier to accept the savior when millions of others have already done so and when the guru exists comfortably only in pictures, paintings, and stories. In real life it is very difficult to have "eyes to see" and "ears to hear" the face and voice of God in an ordinary-looking, even if unusually wise, human being. One can hardly blame the Jews for having been horrified that Jesus declared himself to be the son of God! Considering their history of slavery or occupation by other nations, who among the Jews could have had the faith and imagination to accept that the much-hoped-for Messiah wasn't going to lead the people from their bondage to Roman Rule? Nothing in their own interpretation of their religious teachings and history could have prepared them to meet the "Son of God" in human form.[*]

* It's almost amusing how often throughout the Old Testament God rails against his Chosen People for their stubbornness and refusal to listen to him.

In summary, the power of Jesus or any other *avatar* to forgive sins depends on the depth of attunement of the disciple. Like the woman who touched the robe of Jesus and was healed even though others did the same but were not healed, God seeks those who worship Him "in spirit and in truth."* Attunement cannot be precisely defined but certainly includes our love for God in the form of the guru; it includes the extent to which we live by the precepts and practices given to us by the guru; and the extent to which we serve the guru's work. In these efforts we need not, indeed, cannot of ourselves, attain perfection: that comes through grace. Again, as Krishna so lovingly states in the Bhagavad Gita: "I will make good your deficiencies and render permanent your gains."†

Did Jesus Suffer on the Cross?

Jesus' sacrifice on the cross was dramatic and unique in time and history but the Romans crucified thousands of people in their centuries of rule. This form of death, cruel and painful though it is, was not uncommon during those times.

A God-realized soul has the power of the universe at their command. In the garden of Gethsemane, Jesus did not resist his arrest, yet he stated that he had the power to do so.‡ Unlike you or me, a God-attuned soul can transcend pain in the body at will. I think of the difference between myself and a professional football player. If I were to don the uniform, I would probably not survive the first play before being carried off the field on a stretcher. But a professional football player will play year after year, game after game.

* John 4:23–24
† Bhagavad Gita 9:22
‡ Matt 26:53

I am not saying Jesus did not feel pain. I am saying (actually, Yogananda said) that Jesus consented to feel the pain; he played the drama according to the will of the Father. In *Sanatan Dharma*, the power of a true (*sat*) guru to take on the karma of disciples is a long-standing and well-accepted precept, as discussed earlier in this chapter.

Jesus' sacrifice was for those who are in tune with his will, his teachings, his living presence. The greater the attunement, the greater the grace and blessing. But it was Jesus' gift to those in tune with him to engage fully into the drama, into the *lila* of God, to do the will of the Father. He wasn't simply faking it. The testimony of the crucifixion makes that clear. Had he been faking it his sacrifice would have been false.

But it remains true that for any soul that has achieved cosmic consciousness, being one with the Father/Mother/God, coming back to human form must surely be the greatest sacrifice of all. To be ignored, misunderstood, humiliated, derided, and rejected is the fate of all who come in God's name. The form of rejection by humans is as unique for the *avatar* as each one of us is unique.

Yogananda emphasized that Jesus' life and death assumed the karmic burden primarily of his disciples, whether those with him in the flesh during his earthly life, or those later down through the centuries who were deeply attuned to his omnipresent Spirit.[*]

---

[*] From the Indian perspective, disciples in future centuries, the great ones like St. Francis, were presumably reincarnated souls who had been with Jesus during Jesus' earthly life. Such great saints come to finish off their karma and continue the work of their guru.

Chapter 16

Overcoming *Karma* (Sin)

Is Suffering Sufficient Payment for Past Transgressions?

I DESCRIBED EARLIER HOW SUFFERING CAN BE A PROD TO turn to prayer and to ask the deeper questions of life. But is the experience of suffering, by itself, sufficient expiation for the karmic cause of suffering? If I overeat and suffer gastrointestinal discomfort as a result, is that the end of the karmic story? Isn't it likely that this isn't the first or the last time I overeat? Why did I overeat? Was I inattentive? Preoccupied? If so, why? Was it gluttony? A need to assuage my unhappiness? Even permanent repentance for gluttony isn't going to heal longer-term health issues caused by the habit of gluttony.

Pain or suffering is not, by itself, adequate expiation for either "original sin" or "bad karma." Pain is just one consequence of error. It's a bit like those who imagine that feeling guilty is sufficient to make amends by saying "I'm sorry. I feel terrible for what I have done." "Sin no more," as Jesus counseled several times in the New Testament to those whom he healed and forgave.

Making Amends

In olden times when one king proffers a gift to another
king, the beauty and richness of the gift given is a mark of both
the giving king's own wealth and power as well as a mark of respect and possibly even tribute to the king to whom it is given.
In the archetypal imagery of sacrifice, one sacrifices at the altar
only an animal without blemish; or, in other traditions, a virgin, or some other innocent or prized gift, or perhaps captured
warriors or kings. In other words, a gift is pure if it is precious
(in wealth, beauty, sacredness and/or rarity). If the gift is that
of a person, the person should be innocent or otherwise not
deserving of being sacrificed. In the Old Testament God asked
Abraham to sacrifice (kill) his own, very much-loved (and innocent) son as a sign of faith and obedience. Fortunately for
them both, God's command was only a test which Abraham
passed with the proverbial flags flying.

Acceptance

Although Jesus had no past *karma* (nor original sin) requiring forgiveness, he gave us the example of how to re-
spond to life's trials. Because we are not yet karmically free,
our trials are necessarily our past karma. A devotee may
accept, even welcome, life's tests as gifts from God. A saint
may experience divine bliss even in the midst of suffering.
As Jesus accepted that it was God's will for him to serve as
ransom for the sins of others, we, too, should meet our own
tests with calm acceptance.

In the teachings of yoga, calm acceptance is a way
of life. This is true regardless of one's response, whether that response is passive or proactive. The key is to be

even minded, and even cheerful, under all circumstances.*
Karma means action and reaction. A wise response can
minimize the swing of the pendulum of karma back and
forth with each action and reaction.

Good Deeds, Virtue, Good Karma

We can also proactively make amends in many ways: just
as one who has suffered mental illness becomes a therapist;
a recovering addict, a sponsor; a doubter, a teacher; a glut-
ton, a nutritionist; or a scoffer, a devotee. However, the ef-
fectiveness of a proactive expiation is greatly enhanced if
it is performed in the consciousness of divine duty, with the
power of divine grace, and in the spirit of non-attachment,
acknowledging that God is the true doer of action. Virtuous
action performed in the consciousness of doership may bal-
ance the karmic scales but is not sufficient to redeem our
souls from the "original sin" of egoity: rejection of and separation from God.

Guru's Grace

We've already discussed that attunement to the
guru-savior brings into our life the power of grace to wash
away past karma like a divine tsunami. "Wherefore I say
unto thee, her sins, which are many, are forgiven; for she
loved much."† Love for God in the form of the guru is said,
in *Sanatan Dharma*, to be our raft to salvation.

---

* *Yoga Sutras of Patanjali*, Pada 1, Stanza 2: "*Yogas chitta vritti nirodha*." The state
of yoga is achieved by not reacting to mental, emotional, or physical stimuli. This
does not imply indifference or mindlessness, but equanimity and acceptance of
all as God's loving hand.

† Luke 7:47

Importance of Self-Offering; Self-Sacrifice

In Christianity forgiveness can be washed away by various forms of repentance such as the sacrament of confession, Purgatory, prayers, rituals, penances, and good deeds. In yoga, bad karma can be offset by good karma. That which we have done can, so far as its impact on our soul is concerned, be undone. The wisdom to act wisely is in no small part the gift of grace. But grace is triggered by our openness to it: itself an act. So, while expatiation is good and necessary, it is never enough to raise our consciousness to higher, divine states.

Rev. Martin Luther King, Jr. and Mahatma Gandhi each spoke of the value of accepting unearned suffering with equanimity. In their lives, they modeled Jesus' example by returning love for hatred. They taught the redemptive power of unconditional love to change the hearts and minds of oppressors. Here the emphasis is on *unearned* suffering. One who accepts this illustrates Jesus' counsel to "turn the other cheek."* What does turning the other cheek imply? It means we don't react by fighting back; we don't react with anger; we accept what comes of itself with equanimity in the interest of helping the other person to see for himself the error of his ways.† We act as a mirror so the aggressor can more clearly see himself.

In Hinduism the fire ceremony (called *yagya*) symbolizes an offering or sacrifice given in gratitude and recognition of the divine source of life and bounty. The Bhagavad Gita

---

* Matt 5:38–48

† About suffering abuse, Jesus' counsel still applies but Jesus could never have meant to be a doormat. He was speaking of the courage illustrated by Dr. King or Gandhi. For the oppressed, his counsel surely would include refraining from revenge or anger but he could not have intended to suggest the "victim" accept abuse passively.

describes that the world (universe) is sustained by the enduring cycle of sacrifice: how the sun sacrifices its energy for the earth; rain clouds, their moisture for the fertility of the soil; parents, for their children.

In modern times we talk of delayed gratification. We speak in terms of investing in the future. We take a mortgage in hopes the value of our home will increase above the cost of the mortgage. One who runs a business borrows to build the inventory to increase sales and profits. Even in the mundane business of business, we instinctively know the power of hard work and personal sacrifice. We honor those who gave their lives to defend one's country or freedom. For millennia, kings and their people sacrificed to build monuments to victory or to their gods.

Jesus taught the parable of the sower and the seed: how seed that found fertile soil could produce a hundred-fold in crops.[*]

The Battle of Life: Political Metaphor

It is interesting that the Jews of Jesus' time were expecting a political as well as a spiritual messiah. This was not unreasonable considering Roman occupation and a long history of subjugation in past centuries. A key feature of Jewish history and narrative is their rescue from captivity in Egypt by God (through Moses).

In India, Rama and Krishna, two of India's most beloved *avatars*, were in fact political and spiritual messiahs. Each engaged in victorious warfare against unrighteous enemies. The Hindu "bible," the Bhagavad Gita, which is part of the epic story of the Mahabharata, includes an exhortation to

[*] Mark 4:1–20

do battle with the evil kings. While it is a metaphor for the struggle of the individual soul against delusion, the story has its roots in historical events, similar in this sense, to the Exodus of the Jews.

In the Bhagavad Gita, Krishna explains to his disciple, Arjuna, that whenever virtue declines and vice (unrighteousness) dominates, the Lord incarnates into human form for the upliftment of souls.*

The battle of life is forever portrayed by the world saviors who exhort devotees to strive for Self-realization in God by a combination of self-effort and the redeeming power of grace. Jesus' example to do the will of God at great personal sacrifice is just that: an example. To take it literally and seek martyrdom isn't something that even literal-minded Christian fundamentalists suggest. (And how convenient that they can say that Jesus' sacrifice spared them the trouble.) His example was very dramatic, but perhaps he wanted to make sure the world didn't miss the point. Alas, the world *did* miss the point.

The greatest sacrifice we can offer is not the body, not wealth, not animals, or fruits. It is the ego itself. Even if our life was perfectly virtuous, we would remain imprisoned by the ego. Egoity is the real "original sin" after which all other desires follow all too "naturally." But the world was not ready for that message because the concept of ego didn't exist in common currency until recent times. Instead, for most of the last two thousand years it was the human body that was the definition of the ego. Jesus' statement, "He that loseth his life for My sake will find it," makes the most sense if "life" is understood as "ego" and not the physical body.†

* Gita 4:8
† Matt 10:39

A Tangent Duly Noted

Let me again drift off onto a tangent to share a point of irony noted by my teacher, Swami Kriyananda. Jesus Christ taught his disciples to turn the other cheek but the civilization that embraced those teachings conquered the rest of the world. By contrast, Krishna and Rama engaged in battles for righteousness yet the Hindu culture is known for nonviolence. We in the West were supposed to turn the other cheek while those in the East were supposed to stand up and fight. The irony is admittedly superficial since violence, warfare, and forgiveness exist in all cultures but perhaps the *avatars*, seeing ahead into the future, did what they could to mitigate the tendencies they foresaw in those they came to help. This is yet another reason that God sends new messengers from time to time and to different cultures to help put in-tune souls back on track.*

Another Tangent: Prince and the Pauper — Our Soul's Royal Lineage in God

It is also curious that many of the saviors of humanity have been in some way or another royalty. Buddha was a prince; as were Krishna and Rama. Jesus was of the house of David and was called King of the Jews. Many saints were also highborn. St. Francis was the son of a wealthy merchant. St. Clare was of wealthy parents. In India the path of meditation is called raja yoga, meaning the "royal" path to God, because

---

* Not surprisingly many Christians are inclined to feel "saved by grace" rather than by effort of will. No intelligent reading of the words of Jesus could ever suggest passivity, however. His words are filled with counsel on right behavior and attitude. Life itself demands our effort to survive. The fact that effort alone is insufficient and that divine grace is necessary is the obvious and commonsense precept.

of its one-pointed focus on God. I think (tongue-in-cheek) that the term has a double meaning.

Leading devotees of East and West have often had opportunities to pursue the spiritual path owing to their birth status. Jesus had the wealthy Joseph of Arimathea to provide him the tomb (and one suspects financial support during his life); Yogananda had the self-made millionaire and advanced yogi, James J. Lynn. A study of the lives of saints of East and West would no doubt reveal that most saints and/or key followers formerly held socially privileged status.

In the Bhagavad Gita, Lord Krishna states that those devotees who fail to achieve enlightenment will not incur an evil end but will be able to continue their spiritual pursuit in their next life by achieving noble birth in suitable circumstances. In the context of reincarnation, spiritual advancement requires and reflects degrees of detachment from the ego and its "donkey," the body.* One of the curious attributes of sanctity includes power over nature, and this can include inheriting or being born into circumstances suitable for the pursuit of the spiritual path.

---

* St. Francis famously addressed his body as "Brother Donkey!"

Chapter 17

Jesus and Reincarnation

"**B**E YE THEREFORE PERFECT EVEN AS YOUR FATHER which is in heaven is perfect."* This sentence ends the very long chapter which begins with the inspired Sermon on the Mount, the Beatitudes. That chapter consists of a very long list of "do's" and "don'ts" including the admonition to "turn the other cheek." It makes complete sense that this long list would end and conclude with "be ye therefore perfect."

I say this with a smile, but it begs the question: how can we *ever* become as perfect as God in heaven? For Christians who take the words of Jesus literally (and many claim to do just that), this is pretty scary stuff.† Since Christians admit only to having one human life, they have no choice but to depend almost wholly upon Jesus' death on the cross to affect their eternal salvation at the conclusion of their

---

* Matt 5:48. Considering the history of Judaism with its frequent references to the resurrection and ascension of bodies, who could blame Christians for interpreting the resurrection of Jesus as a promise for their own bodily resurrection (and restoration of ego identity) rather than a declaration of the soul's oneness in God?

† I checked about eight or nine translations of the Bible and all of them used the word "perfect."

less-than-perfect life. And while that is sweet surrender, it seems rather presumptuous, not to mention rather convenient.* Unfortunately, it doesn't really add up. Not only is the efficacy of Jesus' life and suffering in relation to the burden of the sins of millions of Christians one of questionable equivalence, but so too is the grant of eternal freedom or eternal hellfire because of a brief and imperfect span of life.

The doctrine that we are born from nothing and somehow arrive into the world pre-armed with talents, imperfections, and even potential birth defects, and then are subjected to parental, cultural, and environmental influences is, if you think about it, pretty weird. Me perfect? Absurd! On what basis are we handed our unique mixture of characteristics? No parent worthy of the name will insist their child was a clean slate upon which they and environmental influences wrote. It is easily observed that a child comes into this world like a ticking bomb laden with their own preexisting attitudes, interests, and skills.

The doctrine of reincarnation is central, or at least very useful, to a more universal understanding of Christianity, so something must be said. However, my point is not to use persuasive reasoning to convince anyone of it. There are plenty of books on the subject.

Let me begin by pointing out a few shortcomings of believing in our having only one human life.

1. To address the issue of babies or young children who die and haven't had time to merit either heaven or hell, there came into Christianity the concept of Limbo where these little souls get to reside innocently (for eternity!).

---

* See the previous chapter on forgiveness of sins.

2. To deal with the need to mitigate the drastic and irrevocable consequences of eternal heaven or hell, there came into Christian dogma the concept of purgatory, a kind of hellish halfway house to paradise.

3. To deal with the wide range of influences under which souls are born, the idea of "grading on the curve" had to be invented. This takes place in the hairsplitting distinctions between mortal and venial sins and assessing the potential of salvation for souls who have never heard of Jesus.*

Also consider the fate of animals. The one-life dogma requires Christian theology to posit that animals do not have souls because how could they deserve heaven or hell without the power of reason? Anyone who has had a beloved pet or has studied closely animal behavior can see that there's a process akin to reason, as in those wild animals that can use tools, pets who are inventive or creative about escaping or getting into food, or those who follow their owner for hundreds of miles. More than this, there is the self-sacrificing potential demonstrated by many pets and even wild animals; their love, their devotion, and their innumerable humanlike habits and attitudes. A pet can even feel guilty. Can we really say that they have no conscience?

By contrast, reincarnation says that animals have souls and that the evolution of souls up to the human level takes place gradually and by instinct. There is very little, perhaps

* I do not mean to imply that states analogous to "Limbo" or "Purgatory" do not exist, or at least that the need for them isn't valid in the long road of birth, death, and reincarnation. But the need to articulate them arises necessarily out of mercy owing to the one-life dogma. My research suggests that "Limbo" and perhaps "Purgatory" are not de facto dogmas but, rather, they have never been rejected or denied by church authorities or teachings.

no *karma* (sin or merit) accumulated by the soul of an animal. In this way their souls cannot be judged by the same measure as the souls of humans.* Moreover, the yogic teaching is that the human body was specially designed to experience cosmic consciousness. Therefore, *Sanatan Dharma* also recognizes the essential distinction between human and animal states, but it is a matter of degree, not a difference in essential nature.

A common objection to reincarnation is a simple and valid one: why do we not remember our past lives? In fact, quite a few people do! There are countless books that have researched cases of remembered past lives.

Regarding the topic of memory, how much do you remember about your thoughts ten minutes ago? Or what you did three days ago? A week ago? How much of your childhood do you remember? Consider the consequences if you *did* remember not just one past life but many? You would be so burdened by memory that you would be paralyzed. Forgetfulness is a gift so that with each rebirth we have an opportunity to start over. But our new life isn't a blank slate. Our past actions create in us a freight train's worth of tendencies, unfulfilled desires, talents, shortcomings, and unresolved relationships. At least we can deal with the deck of karma cards we've dealt ourselves without being burdened

* Just as the one-life teaching necessitates concepts of Limbo and Purgatory, so does the "God-became-the-creation" teaching require all things to have souls (or some level of consciousness). Technically, it isn't so much that a rock has a soul as a rock contains the innate intelligence sufficient to form and "act like" a rock. Debates as to when the soul emerges are beyond my "paygrade" and much can and has been said on the subject, but without practical value. God's reflected intention and intelligence can be seen from stars to atoms but I suppose a "soul" to be a "soul" must have some budding measure of self-awareness which is difficult to imagine in a rock. But that's just my opinion. I concede therefore the efficacy of Limbo and Purgatory in some measure.

by the memory of what we did to deserve them.* The more practical question in our current life, then, is how to deal with the facts as they presently exist.

Swami Kriyananda did extensive research on the topic and shared the following in his autobiography *The New Path*. This is from the chapter entitled "Reincarnation."

> On the subject of reincarnation, Indian philosophy seems to be at odds with the Christian teachings. In fact, however, this doctrine is denied only in prevailing *interpretations* of the Bible, and not by the Bible itself. Reincarnation is not an *un-Christian* teaching. Nor, for that matter, is it an un-Jewish one. It was taught by some of the great early Christian Fathers, including Origen (A.D. 185–254), who claimed he'd received it in an unbroken tradition 'from apostolic times.' It was not until five centuries after Christ, in 553 A.D. at the Second Council of Constantinople, that this doctrine was finally removed from Christian dogma. The anathema pronounced against it was delivered owing to certain political maneuverings, and was less an outcome of theological purism. Scholars have recently discovered that Pope Vigilius, though present in Constantinople at that time, took no part in pronouncing the anathema, and in fact boycotted the Council itself altogether.

> Numerous Biblical passages support belief in reincarnation. The doctrine of rebirth may be found, subsequent to Biblical times, in Jewish as well as in Christian traditions.

---

* Jesus gave this perfect counsel to those who are overly curious about their past lives: Matt 6:34: "Sufficient unto the day is the evil thereof." (Deal with what is in front of you. Let go for now the "Why?")

Rabbi Manasseh ben Israel (1604–1657 A.D.), Jewish theologian and statesman, wrote, 'The belief or the doctrine of the transmigration of souls is a firm and infallible dogma accepted by the whole assemblage of our church with one accord, so that there is none to be found who dares to deny it. . . . The truth of it has been incontestably demonstrated by the Zohar, and all the books of the Kabalists' and while modern Jews generally reject this doctrine, rabbis familiar with the spiritual traditions of Judaism do not endorse that rejection.

Reincarnation is endorsed in the *Shulhan Oruch*, which is the major book of laws in the Torah. A student for the rabbinate in Israel once sent me several supportive quotations from this book, including these words from the *Sha'ar Hatsiyune*, letter 6vav: 'That soul will be sent time and time again to this world until he does what God wants him to do.' The student said that his rabbi, after reading this letter, could no longer deny the doctrine of reincarnation.

Rabbi Abraham Yehoshua, a Hasidic master who died in 1825, spoke of ten lives that he had lived previously, concluding, 'and so I was sent forth again and again in order to perfect my love. If I succeed this time, I shall never return again.'

Among famous Westerners who have subscribed to this doctrine, the German philosopher Schopenhauer wrote: 'Were an Asiatic to ask me for a definition of Europe, I should be forced to answer him: It is that part of the world which is haunted by the incredible delusion that man was created out of nothing, and that his present birth is his first entrance into life.' Voltaire wrote, 'It is not more surprising to be born twice than once.' The British philosopher Hume stated that reincarnation is 'the only system to which Philosophy can so much as hearken.'

Also consider this excerpt from Yogananda's autobiography with examples from the Bible:

"Thus, it becometh us to fulfill all righteousness."* In these words, to John the Baptist, and in asking John to baptize him, Jesus was acknowledging the divine rights of his guru.

From a reverent study of the Bible from an Oriental viewpoint, and from intuitional perception, I am convinced that John the Baptist was, in past lives, the guru of Christ. There are numerous passages in the Bible which infer that John and Jesus in their last incarnations were, respectively, Elijah and his disciple Elisha. (These are the spellings in the Old Testament. The Greek translators spelled the names as Elias and Eliseus; they reappear in the New Testament in these changed forms.)

The very end of the Old Testament is a prediction of the reincarnation of Elijah and Elisha: "Behold, I will send you Elijah the prophet before the coming of the great and dreadful day of the Lord."† Thus John (Elijah), sent "before the coming . . . of the Lord," was born slightly earlier to serve as a herald for Christ. An angel appeared

* Matt 3:15
† Malachi 4:5

to Zacharias the father to testify that his coming son John would be no other than Elijah (Elias).

"But the angel said unto him, Fear not, Zacharias: for thy prayer is heard; and thy wife Elisabeth shall bear thee a son, and thou shalt call his name John . . . and many of the children of Israel shall he turn to the Lord their God. and he shall go before him* in *the spirit and power of Elias*, to turn the hearts of the fathers to the children, and the disobedient to the wisdom of the just; to make ready a people prepared for the Lord."

Jesus twice unequivocally identified Elijah (Elias) as John: "Elias is come already, and they knew him not. . . . Then the disciples understood that he spake unto them of John the Baptist."† Again, Christ says: "For all the prophets and the law prophesied until John, and if ye will receive it, this is Elias, which was for to come."‡

When John denied that he was Elias (Elijah),§ he meant that in the humble garb of John he came no longer in the outward elevation of Elijah the great guru. In his former incarnation he had given the "mantle" of his glory and his spiritual wealth to his disciple Elisha. "Elisha said, I pray thee, let a double portion of thy spirit be upon me and he said, thou hast asked a hard thing: nevertheless, if thou see me when I am taken from thee, it shall be so unto thee . . . and he took the *mantle* of Elijah that fell from him."¶

* Luke 1:13–17
† Matt 17:12–13
‡ Matt 11:13–14
§ John 1:21
¶ II Kings 2:9–14

The roles became reversed, because Elijah-John was no longer needed to be the ostensible guru of Elisha-Jesus, now perfected in divine realization.

When Christ was transfigured on the mountain[*] it was his guru Elias, with Moses, whom he saw. Again, in his hour of extremity on the cross, Jesus cried out the divine name: *Eli, Eli, lama sabachthani,* "that is to say, My God, my God, why hast thou forsaken me? Some of them that stood there, when they heard that, said, 'this man calleth for Elias. . . . Let us see whether Elias will come to save him.'"[†]

Here is one more example taken from the Gospel of John[‡] in which Jesus meets a blind man.

1 and as Jesus passed by, he saw a man which was blind from his birth.

2 and his disciples asked him, saying, Master, who did sin, this man, or his parents, that he was born blind?

3 Jesus answered, Neither hath this man sinned, nor his parents: but that the works of God should be made manifest in him.

If we look at this incident, the man was blind *since birth*. The disciples ask him whether he was blind since birth because of *his* sin or that of his parents. Now how could this man have sinned *before* his birth unless the conversation assumed, without comment, reincarnation as a fact?

In the earlier quotes from Jesus such as "Elias has come already," and in this story of the blind man, Jesus had an

[*] Matt 17:3
[†] Matt 27:46–49
[‡] John 9:1–3

opportunity to speak openly of reincarnation, either to endorse or condemn it, but his response was oblique, or he
sidestepped it altogether.

In these examples I attempt to show that there is not a
simple and obvious answer to the question of whether reincarnation is or is not taught in the Bible, in Judaism, or even
in the history of the early Christians. My purpose is to reveal
how it might be possible that future Christians will "discover"
the doctrine of reincarnation in their own spiritual tradition.

I am not a scholar of Jewish history and teachings, but
it seems to me that the teaching of the "transmigration of
souls" was not a pronounced dogma of Judaism then or now.
Judaism, I have read, is not focused on dogma or credo but,
to an important extent, on obedience to the law as God's
chosen people. The Old Testament contains references to the
afterlife in relation to the resurrection of the dead, meaning
in bodily form. In the continuum of Judaic belief and expectation, it makes perfect sense that Jesus would have been
resurrected bodily after his crucifixion.[*]

An opinion I received from my teacher, Swami
Kriyananda, and one that makes sense to me considering
human nature, follows this line of thinking: reincarnation
was not taught nor agreed upon in Judaism in the first century A.D. There would have been little point in introducing
a teaching whose impact might likely have had the effect of
weakening an aspirant's motivation. Civilization at that time
was deeply materialistic, brutal, and sensual, and the teaching of reincarnation would be merely an excuse to postpone
the need for virtue. Even in the current age it doesn't always

---

[*] Of the two main religious groups at the time of Jesus, the Sadducees did not
believe in the afterlife.

have the desired effect. Swami Kriyananda told a story of a woman overheard leaving a talk on reincarnation saying "Oh boy! We get to come back!"

"Fire and brimstone" was a useful concept in Christianity for upwards two thousand years. But is it still? Are most Christians today motivated by fear of God (or of hell)? Or is love of God (not fear) a more pure and useful motivation in the twenty-first century? Did not Jesus' message include forgiveness and love?

Expediency, not the truth of the teaching, is what I believe happened in Christianity with relation to reincarnation.* In the East where belief in and discussion of reincarnation was as common as a discussion of the weather among farmers, reincarnation was a moot issue. But for Christianity, as mentioned earlier, ignoring reincarnation necessitated some pretzel-like dogmas such as Limbo and Purgatory to answer some challenging ethical questions.

Reincarnation: Will I be a Spider in My Next Life?

I won't spend time defining reincarnation, but there are many, many misconceptions about how it works. For one thing, the form you get at your next birth is not arbitrary. You won't just happen to be a spider next time.†

---

* I see a parallel in the abandonment of ritual animal sacrifices by the Jews which had otherwise been practiced up until the destruction of the temple in Jerusalem in A.D. 70. Deeply embedded teachings and practices *can* change, even abruptly.

† Swami Kriyananda taught that Yogananda said if a human behaves like "an animal" he might end up becoming one in the next life. Yogananda apparently also taught that if the same soul continues in the downward spiral of bestial behavior he could even become a germ. But this is highly unlikely. Usually, the soul returns to human form after a time or two as a dog, cat, or some other form. How often I have looked into the eyes of some pet only to see a human soul trapped there, even if it be but temporarily.

Reincarnation is the necessary corollary to the law of karma: action and reaction. As St. Paul wrote to the Galatians: "Be not deceived, God is not mocked. For whatsoever a man soweth, that he shall also reap."* There are several references in Revelations that go something like: "To him that overcometh will I make a pillar in the house of God, and he will go out no more."†

In the East it is taught that one's thoughts at the time of death can influence one's next life. Paramhansa Yogananda addressed this in his teachings as well. The main point I wish to make is that reincarnation follows the line of thought and action that we ourselves initiate. Our stay in heaven or in hell after death is temporary.‡ We come back into human form so long as material desires (or fears) compel us to do so.§ We rest in the afterlife if it is deserved or needed. We continue with the process of birth, life, death, and reincarnation until we rebel at the recollection of the "anguishing monotony" of endless rounds of rebirth and seek freedom in the transcendent realm of God-consciousness: the very essence of our own soul. The state of union with God is a state beyond the "many mansions of my Father's house."⁵ The heavenly spheres are but steppingstones to God-realization because God is beyond name and form and time and place.

In conclusion, the command by Jesus "to be perfect" can only find meaning in the context of karma and reincarnation.

* Galatians 6:7
† Revelations 3:12, e.g.
‡ We'll come to the subject of heaven and hell soon enough.
§ An excellent description of the process of death, heaven, hell, and rebirth can be found in Paramhansa Yogananda's life story: *Autobiography of a Yogi* in the chapter "The Resurrection of Sri Yukteswar."
⁵ John 14:2

These twin teachings align harmoniously with our scientific mindset of cause and effect as well as with Jesus' teaching of God's mercy and love for the creation and all creatures. Not only does Jesus ask us to turn the other cheek and accept offense seven times seventy, but God, for whom time is not a boundary, has given to us countless incarnations to unmask the Creator behind the creation.

Chapter 18

Oh Hell, Let's Talk About It

MAYBE IT'S TIME TO DROP THE LITERAL INTER-
pretation of heaven or hell as eternal. After all,
Jesus changed the Mosaic law in respect to divorce, didn't he?* It is easy "as hell" to say that we humans
find the whole idea of eternal reward or punishment an
astonishingly illogical and unfair dogma. For example,
if I am given only one life and I kill someone it seems
fair that the consequences are forever. But if I am given
one life and I happen to grow up in morally disadvan-
taged circumstances and make a few missteps, now I am
in hell forever. How is that fair? Not so in the world view
of reincarnation.

Looking at it from the perspective of cause and effect,
eternal consequences could arguably be the result of having
only one life, because with only one life no opportunities
exist to redeem one's actions. I can see therefore how "one
life" and "eternity" go together while, by contrast, reincarnation and progressive awakening into Self-realization go
together. Given a choice the latter is more just, merciful, and

* Matt 5:17

124

illustrative of divine love. Even Jesus' own words can be seen to affirm, or at least not deny, the teaching of reincarnation. And great saints and *avatars* have affirmed it for millennia, as do a large percentage of people today. I'm sure you can guess where I sit on the question.

Cause and effect and the moving pendulum of duality rule the known universe. Why wouldn't they also rule the heavens of the afterlife above? In *Sanatan Dharma*, cessation of motion exists only in God the Father-Spirit beyond the vibratory creation. Heaven, as is commonly thought of, is the astral and causal spheres of creation as described earlier in this book. They are as much in eternal flux as the material universe.

There's no denying that in our English language Bible, Jesus is quoted as using words like "eternal" or "everlasting" in relation to both heaven and hell. Even on earth we may experience idyllic times or pain and suffering that feel like they will never end. But they do end.

Heaven and Hell on Earth

A popular story from Greek mythology aptly depicts the hell of entrenched habits. The character Sisyphus is endlessly pushing a boulder up the hill only to have it roll down again. Such is a metaphor for the hell on earth caused by our overindulgence in the vices and habits of the material world. The law of diminishing returns operates to bring less and less satisfaction, even as we are imprisoned by the force of habit to endless repetition. Like Sisyphus, the sense-addict lives in a kind of hell from which there appears to be no escape. Material delusions such as the obvious ones of alcohol, sex, money, fame, and beauty must be continually experienced until their repetition brings to us to boredom, disease, emotional devastation, despair and, finally, to the determination to escape their prison. Reincarnation is the same, but on a larger scale. It is a form of prison and therefore a kind of hell.[*]

Virtue is the "heaven" on earth in that it brings cooling, satisfying clarity, calmness, and wisdom to every aspect of one's life. While we might imagine that freedom means we can do what we want, if, by the repetition of our desires, we find ourselves imprisoned in destructive habits, we cannot say we are free. Freedom, it has been well said, is not the freedom to do what we want, but the wisdom and the strength to do what is right. Developing good habits requires self-discipline.

Some of the results of virtue are peace of mind, a clear conscience, harmonious relationships, good health, the respect of others, an esteemed reputation, and nobility of character. Far from diminishing returns, the fruits of virtue expand exponentially. It is also true that the real heaven of union with God that awaits our souls exceeds the satisfaction that human virtue brings, for virtue is founded on reason and the Golden Rule. The real heaven is the bliss of God-consciousness and divine bliss, which Paramhansa Yogananda said, is "ever-new."

Personal vice or virtue aside, one does not have to go very far on this planet Earth to find hell, or, for that matter, heaven. We do not have to die to find them. Just read the headlines. Heaven and hell exist between our ears and in our hearts.[†] The angelic powers and the satanic forces which vie for willing workers find plenty of volunteers.

---

[*] I've sometimes joked that the reason to seek the end of reincarnation (union with God) is not to have come back and be a teenager again!

[†] This is not a denial of their transcendental existence.

Paramhansa Yogananda told a story of a farmer he met in Washington State when he went to a farmhouse to purchase some cherries. They talked lightheartedly for a bit, but Yogananda intuitively felt that the man carried a burden in his heart. The farmer revealed his unhappiness about his wayward son. The farmer feared that his son was doomed to eternal damnation. Yogananda asked the farmer whether he'd like to do something about his son. When the farmer assented and asked what it was, Yogananda suggested that they wait for the son to come home late at night (presumably drunk), and when he arrived, "We'll tie him up and throw him into that large oven you have!" The farmer was outraged at the idea. Yogananda asked that if he, an ordinary human father, could not do this to his wayward son, how then, could God the Father? The farmer broke down in tears and understood immediately.

There's no logic worthy of living except the logic of the heart. The soul's intuitive knowing silently tells us to discard forever (pun intended) the teaching of eternal damnation. We can say that the dogma of Christianity was simply an understandable interpretation of the words of Jesus (and of some words in the Old Testament) that served its purpose for the epoch we have come through. Like animal sacrifice, maybe it's time we let it go.

Chapter 19

Do Spiritual
Teachings Change?

WE HAVE JUST CONSIDERED THE QUESTION OF whether Jesus taught the doctrine of reincarnation and whether he intended heaven and hell to be places of eternal rest or damnation. Those who read Jesus' words and cling to them with determined faith, might do well to consider the evolution of the very teachings that Jesus said he came to fulfill.* Read all the laws and commands that God gives to Moses, for example. There are 613 rules, most of which are in the negative. Many involve detailed instructions on how to make an animal sacrifice that is pleasing to the Lord. Many have to do with ritual cleanliness like not sitting where a woman who is on her monthly period has sat.

Consider the verbal exchange Jesus had with the Pharisees in the Gospel of Mark.† The Pharisees are baiting Jesus and ask him the question "Is it lawful for a husband to divorce his wife?" Jesus wisely shoots back a question to them: "What did

* Matt 5:17
† Mark 10:1–5

128

Moses command you?" The Pharisees explained that Moses taught that a husband must make a written declaration in order to divorce his wife. My interpretation of Moses' law is that this made it seemingly easy for a husband to get rid of his wife. So perhaps it was even in Jesus' time a precept of questionable moral value. Whatever the case may have been, Jesus was quick to critique the law but not Moses for having given it. Instead, Jesus' response was to say that "For the hardness of your heart he (Moses) wrote you this precept."

Jesus takes it further to affirm the sanctity of marriage.* My point here, however, is that Jesus openly changed, indeed, refined, one of the important laws of Moses. In the gospel of Matthew Jesus introduced numerous refinements to Jewish law clarifying, as but one example, that adultery takes place first in the mind and heart and only secondarily, if at all, physically.† When Jesus healed on the Sabbath and was accused of violating the laws of the Sabbath, he similarly clarified and refined the deeper meaning and importance of the Sabbath.

Jesus thus proposed new standards of ethical behavior. Teachings, in other words, *do* change, and they are best changed by those high souls who come for that purpose according to the needs of those for whom the *avatar* is sent. Since we are speaking here of the laws of Moses, how many

---

* Paramhansa Yogananda acknowledged that in modern times divorce is all too common and all too easily accomplished. He clarified Jesus' strong words upholding the sanctity of marriage to say that most modern marriages are not spiritual marriages because they are based on superficial attractions. He stated that Jesus' teaching here applies more appropriately to a marriage of soul qualities wherein two souls are drawn to one another based on their higher aspirations and not owing to a temporary infatuation-based physical attraction, personal convenience, or material goals.

† Matt Chapter 5

of those hundreds of laws are still observed by Jews who consider themselves devout and loyal to their faith? On what basis do they ignore "an eye for an eye" and numberless other commandments? Surely, they are sincere, and surely, they have found righteous justification for the changes they have made.

When you consider the changes that Jesus and his apostles made in reformatting Judaism to include Gentiles you simply must admit: "Hey, things change." In the Old Testament God said that the penalty for failure to circumcise was death! The apostles decided to let that one go. Failure to observe the Sabbath had its severe punishments. I can imagine God Almighty saying, "What? You did *what*?!" I doubt there is a Christian to be found anywhere who feels Christianity should have kept the law of circumcision! If the apostles and later church leaders (and not just Jesus himself) found a way to discard such a powerful body of religious laws, then I urge Christians to have the courage to take a fresh look at those teachings which no longer ring true.

What was the justification for these important changes that they made? Simple: a great prophet had come from God to "fulfill" the prior covenant by taking it to its next level of refinement.

Christian dogma gets a great deal of mileage out of insisting that Jesus made a new covenant with his people. If God made a covenant with Abraham, then later, with Moses and if Christians believe yet another covenant has been created through Jesus Christ, then who cannot help but ask, given the desperate spiritual needs of our times, is it time for a new covenant? Maybe this is a reason that Yogananda called his teachings a "new dispensation?" He also termed his work the Second Coming of Christ.

Can Christians let go of the concept of eternal damnation and view it as a metaphor or even a psychological reality? Is it time to look more deeply at reincarnation? Are Christians ready to accept multiple Christ-like saviors throughout history? When will Catholics concede their desperate need for and the righteousness of having women (and married) priests?

All human activities, beliefs, and customs evolve. The basic precepts, like the Golden Rule and the two great commandments that constitute the essence of the teachings of both the Old and New Testament survive, but the forms they can take are subject to evolution just as we see in nature and in our own lives as we learn and grow.*

The changes in the teachings of all religions are too numerous and drastic to even begin to list. As only a few in the beginning recognized Jesus as the Messiah, we cannot blithely assume that very many will be open to important changes in the twenty-first century. Perhaps it is time to ask some important, if challenging, questions.

Who says we'll recognize Jesus in his next incarnation? How will we know if that person *is* Jesus? Will it matter?†

Our times are not those of Jesus. The rapid and global expansion of ideas and the intermixture of religions holds the promise of a larger number of eyes to see and ears to hear. I hope, therefore, that Christians will be more open to Jesus' second coming and what he will say, do, or how he will appear.

* Matt 22:36–40; Old Testament is Deuteronomy 6:5 and Leviticus 19:18. "Thou shalt love the Lord thy God with all thy heart, mind, soul, and strength. And the second is like unto the first: Thou shalt love thy neighbor as thyself."

† "Those who do not learn from history are doomed to repeat it." George Santayana. My suspicion is that change will come "from below." By this I mean not from religious authorities but from the people. This possibility is far more in tune and possible in present day culture than it was in Jesus' time.

Chapter 20

Ego and Divine Union

I HAVE MADE NUMEROUS REFERENCES TO THE SOUL'S destiny in God. As described earlier, it has many names. In Christianity these include terms such as mystical marriage, union, salvation, and heaven. In *Sanatan Dharma* some commonly used terms are *moksha*, cosmic consciousness, and *samadhi*. But what is this state in relation to our current state of individual, egoic awareness? In God does the ego continue its separate existence or is the ego dissolved like a drop of water into a lake? There are two fundamental interpretations:

> **The ego survives forever.** In the Abrahamic faiths the soul's reward for good behavior is to go to heaven for eternity and remain separate from God, perhaps strumming a harp. In some versions we are reunited with our physical body, whereas in other versions the nature of our "body" is not described. In both cases, the "I" survives, and we enjoy Paradise in the presence of God for eternity. It sounds fine to have been saved from eternal damnation if that's the alternative, but it also sounds potentially boring.

The ego is obliterated. In some versions of Eastern religions, the ego is destroyed, and we merge back into God (or into No-Thingness) and there is no continuation of individual consciousness and thus no continued separate existence. The problem with this one is that it affronts my fundamental instinct to survive. I'm not sure I want to be obliterated.

With characteristic wit and wisdom Paramhansa Yogananda asks, "What if Infinity contains both?" This is the epitome of what I call "Both-And." What if the memory of being identified with the many physical bodies, the astral body, and the causal body is forever retained in the Infinite consciousness of God? At the same time, after our salvation, there is no longer an "I" that identifies itself as a separate entity associated with any of these past lives, bodies, or personalities?* What if merging in God takes place when we sever our identification with a limited self? What is "killed" is not our conscious self-awareness but only our false sense of identity with that limited self (the ego). Paramhansa Yogananda offers us the idea that our past lives are like fictional characters in a novel. They seem real to us when we are engrossed in the reading but fade away once the book is closed.

On the one hand, our souls are like a drop of water that merges back into the Ocean of Consciousness, and on the other hand, the memory of countless lifetimes remains as a present reality in the Infinity of that Ocean. The drop of water that merges into the ocean hasn't changed. Yogananda suggested that if Jesus Christ were reincarnated

* Three bodies as taught in India: physical, astral, and causal.

into another body, a devotee could still call Jesus Christ to the fore in vision or in human form because in the omnipresent consciousness of God, Jesus Christ lives now and forever.

It is nearly impossible for us to imagine infinity or the consciousness of God, but we do get hints. Consider this famous statement by Jesus: "Before Abraham was, I AM." The phrase I AM suggests a continuity of self-awareness. By asserting that this I AM existed before Abraham we have a hint of Jesus' consciousness transcending space and time. In the New Testament there is an account of Jesus being transfigured and seen by his disciples in Jesus' etheric or astral body together with those of Moses and Elijah. Moses and Elijah lived many centuries before Jesus' time and thus, again, we see a hint of the continuity of the soul's existence.

Swami Kriyananda once made the bold statement that "we are as old as God" because we are sparks of the divine flame. Although God hides behind the appearance of creation, He is playing all the parts of the drama.

Over countless lifetimes we go up and down the ladder, and in and out of our Father's many mansions. Between each human incarnation we reside in the astral (heavenly) realms where we may be aware, or asleep in a dreamlike state.

There is a story in the New Testament in which Jesus is given a riddle to solve by the Sadducees. They ask a question about the afterlife state: if a woman had been married several times on earth (owing to having been widowed more than once), which husband would be hers in heaven?* Jesus scoffs that they don't know what they are talking about because in heaven there is no marriage.

* Matt 22:23–29

But Aren't I Unique?

Notwithstanding this both-and proposition regarding our expansion of consciousness beyond a limited identification with form, Yogananda also stated that "each atom in creation is inextinguishably dowered with individuality." So far as I know, Yogananda did not expound on the nature of this individuality. We commonly say that each snowflake is unique. I don't know how we know that, but if it is true, I suppose this offers us a hint. We can say that our body in place and time and movement is unique; our thoughts at any moment are unique to that moment; and so on. But I don't believe that's what he meant by individuality. My limited understanding is that our individuality possesses a unique core of vibrational attributes, though I am not wholly sure what those are. Perhaps vibrational attributes are a rainbow-like mixture of artistic, inventive, logical, devotional, philosophical, and energetic qualities. In addition, this rich recipe might interact with other characteristics such as being outgoing or introspective. I'm speculating, but I am certain that our uniqueness is not merely the accumulation of karma that is heaped upon the soul over its many lifetimes. This uniqueness is some aspect of what is retained in the infinite presence of God even when all lesser identifications have been dissolved in divine Bliss.

Soulmates?

Yogananda made a passing reference to our monad soul being cleaved in twain upon our first creation. Before we can achieve final liberation from all forms, duality, and karma, we must reunite with our other half, our soulmate. However, he made it clear that he was not talking in romantic terms. Swami Kriyananda warned us not to go looking for our soulmate, but to focus our devotion on God and guru, through whose grace we will find what and who we need when the time is right. Our reunion evidently is not one of physical form but of consciousness. Referring to the above discussion about our unique qualities, I imagine the soulmate to be those opposite qualities, which when united, free us from all qualities. But as I said, I'm speculating.

Where in Heaven is Heaven?

There are several parables by Jesus that begin with "The kingdom of heaven is like . . ." Yogananda suggests that Jesus used the term "heaven" in two different ways. Only the context of the metaphor or parable reveals which meaning is intended. The first and commonly assumed meaning is the residence in the astral world where souls go temporarily after death. But the second and deeper meaning is the state of union with God.

The parable of the mustard seed is an example of Jesus' use of the term "heaven" to describe the state of cosmic consciousness.* It is fine to describe the astral worlds as a great tree sheltering souls who are residing there, but why the part of the parable that explains that this great tree starts from a tiny seed? That tiny seed that grows into a large tree fits the analogy of the individual soul's gradual ascension from ego consciousness to infinite consciousness! Those who live in the consciousness of God are like a great tree that gives sheltering love and acceptance to all creatures.

* Matt 13:31–32

Such is the life of the great ones like Jesus, Buddha, Krishna, and others.

As devotees expand their consciousness beyond the ego and body to embrace all life they grow upward toward Infinity and their souls merge with God. But in this merger, they are not destroyed because they have merely come home. Nothing is lost in God. This final state is both the destruction of the soul's ego identity and the full realization of the soul's unique and indestructible individuality.* The soul, like God, now requires no body or form, though, for one reason or another, it might take on a form temporarily. As all things exist in the eternal *now* of God, so does the soul exist in the boundless state of God's consciousness.

How can such a state be explained in words? If I explain what "joy" is, would that help someone who has never experienced it? Will eternal bliss end up being boring? Yogananda tells us that bliss is "ever-new." He appended those two words to the definition of divine bliss for this very reason. I guess we must wait and see for ourselves and be open to accepting the testimony of those who have achieved it.

How can union with God be anything but the greatest fulfillment? What could possibly be lost in God? While it is fine to say the ego is destroyed, the more correct view is that the ego expands into Infinity, back into the only reality there is: God. Life is a journey of self-expansion from childhood to adulthood. A child grows into an adult and perhaps becomes a great emperor while the seedling of the awakening soul grows into a "tree" of Self-realization to become one with all life.

* Yogananda stated that like each snowflake, each soul appearing out of God in creation bears a uniqueness that is not the same as the personality that forms like layers of earth covering the gold of our soul.

Chapter 21

Your Heaven or Mine?

I FIND IT CURIOUS THAT IN THE WEST SAINTS DEPICT the heavenly realms in terms befitting *their* beliefs,* and in the East the same thing happens. Will the real heaven please stand up?

Christian mystics report seeing heavenly hosts praising the Lord: "Holy, Holy, Holy." And both the Old Testament and St. John in Revelations describe a vision of heaven as containing, among other things, four beasts with eyes all around and twenty-four elders before the throne.† Saints have testified that they have been shown souls in purgatory and in hell, as well as in heaven itself. Jesus and Mary and archangels and saints appear to the Christian mystics in regular procession. I personally find that wonderful, but what is a Buddhist to make of it?

In the East, the vision of "above" is far more impersonal. Yogananda's masterful poem "Samadhi" describes the experience of cosmic consciousness in terms not unlike the famous

---

* Various Christian saints have described seeing people in heaven or in hell, for example. Admitting these astral "mansions" is a given; it's the eternal judgment that is in question.

† Revelations 4:4–8

sequence in the movie *2001: A Space Odyssey*. The poem describes the sheaths (*koshas*) of creation, and it portrays a journey upward but also backwards through the processes of creation. Even Arjuna's vision of Krishna in the Bhagavad Gita, while more poetic, is nonetheless a mind-blowing experience for him.*

So, which is it: personal or impersonal? Is it subjective? Of course. There is nothing more subjective than consciousness itself. Some people say that if you can imagine it, it already exists somewhere. Where do ideas come from? You don't really know because they just appear out of nowhere in your head. Not unlike the Big Bang explanation for how the universe began. No one knows where it came from. They posit a "point of singularity," but all they can really say is the whole universe must have come from, yup, nowhere. However, as the wife of a friend of mine likes to say to him, "Some of your ideas are better than others." The mind of God is infinitely creative.

If God is, as we have been told by none other than an authority like Jesus Christ, "a Spirit," it means that God has no form, no definitions. There is nothing you can pin God down with!

Yogananda taught that a deeply devoted devotee can call out into vision, or even into flesh and blood, the form of any great saint or master, even if that soul has taken on a new incarnation into human form. The Infinity of Truth contains all things as a present reality, or so we are given to imagine.

* In Chapter 11 of the Bhagavad Gita, the disciple Arjuna asks his guru, Lord Krishna, to grant him a vision of the Lord in the cosmic state. There follows a poetic description of omnipresence that takes its place among the great pieces of literature throughout the world that attempt to describe the indescribable vision of God as the Creator.

In the Bhagavad Gita, Krishna speaks straight up and says God will come to a devotee in any form the devotee holds dear.* Swami Kriyananda would joke that if you worship the Sacred Alligator, God will come to you in that form (and probably eat you up). We should have some common sense, however, and see that some forms are more in tune with higher reality than other forms. Our life experiences, both mundane and transcendental, come to us in forms that are personal to us. This is not a denial of objective reality but a recognition that objective reality proceeds from consciousness: not ours alone, but God's consciousness. As sparks of the Infinite consciousness, we also dream and play, and hence create for ourselves a reality taken from the fabric of the great Dream of God.

God is a Spirit and has no form. The various personal forms of approaching God are necessarily part of the creation itself and thus necessarily dual in nature. Thus, our relationship with God takes the "I-Thou" form so beloved by devotees everywhere. Though not personal in anthropomorphic terms, even the abstract forms of God such as inner light or the sound of *AUM* or Amen are products of duality. So also, of course, is the divine but human form of the true guru-savior such as Jesus Christ. God has taken all forms of creation and we must not therefore limit the form through which divine energy, intelligence, love or bliss might come to us according to our own nature and needs.[†‡] Approaching God in form — as the guru in human form, or a deity, or even

* Bhagavad Gita 4:11

† See an earlier footnote about the theologian, Thomas of Acquinas. Thomas had an experience of God in the formless state and he declared that all he had written, including his Summae Theologica, were as nothing.

‡ Bhagavad Gita 12:1–5

as an attribute of God such as love, peace, or wisdom — is the natural way by which we ascend towards the Ultimate.

This book isn't about Hindu saints, but I can assure you that there are innumerable stories of devotees who are blessed with visions of, say, Krishna, who later are guided by a guru to go beyond that beloved form into the formless state. Thus, not surprisingly, Buddhism, founded by a Hindu, posits not just the formless state as the ultimate state, but a state of no-thing-ness.* What Buddha said and what his disciples teach are, as in the case of Jesus Christ, two different things. But this book is not about Buddhism. The problem with the ultimate reality being nothing is that almost no one is going to be inspired to be nothing. Self-preservation is a basic instinct and doesn't seem, to me at least, to have anything to do with the particulars of my ego-ness.

Dark Night of the Soul

Where does the testimony of saints regarding the "dark night of the soul" enter our soul's journey? Might it be that the ego must confront what seems to be its own destruction before it can enter the kingdom of cosmic consciousness (union with God)?

Yogananda stated that Moses was a Self-realized master and *avatar*. But as the one who led the Israelites out of bondage, he symbolized the role of the enlightened ego. He was thus symbolically prevented from entering the Promised

---

* Of Oneness, no two words suffice. It has been called the darkless dark; the lightless light; the Void. "It" can only be described by what *it* is *not*. When there's no I-Thou and only One, how can "one" describe "it?" Buddha chose silence and Silent *it is*. So this is not a criticism of Buddhism.

Land because the ego, which leads us from bondage and co-
operates with grace in the journey of Self-realization, must
die before the soul, the "moon of my delight who know'est no
wane" rises in the sky of consciousness.*

The 23rd psalm offers encouragement to the faithful
during the soul's dark night: "yea though I walk through the
valley of death, I will fear no evil: for thou art with me; thy
rod and thy staff they comfort me." When St. Anthony of
the Desert was assailed by demons, Jesus at last appeared to
him and reassured him, "Anthony, I was always with you."
Although nothing dies in God, for in God all things exist, the
soul must come to know this from deep within itself. Jesus
addresses this struggle between the soul and the ego when
he said, "For whosoever will save his life shall lose it; and
whosoever will lose his life for my sake shall find it.†

Heaven and Eternal Life

What is this "eternal life" so often spoken of by Jesus?
Elsewhere I quoted Yogananda as defining the ego as "the
soul identified with the body." To the extent that we identify ourselves with the body, we "die" because the body dies.
Identifying with the body includes our attachment to pleasure, comfort, recognition, or material success. These are experiences that come and go and cannot be made permanent.
Eternal life then is identification with that which does not
die: the soul. If you prefer, try the term "self-awareness" for
the word "soul." The soul is the essential reality — a spark

---

* A quotation, perhaps paraphrased, from Omar Khayyam's *Rubaiyat*.
Paramhansa Yogananda gives a commentary on the *Rubaiyat* that is deeply re-
vealing showing that Omar, too, was a great sage and master.
† Matt 16:25

of the Infinite consciousness of God — it cannot die. We do not have to "kill" the body to achieve immortality. The soul exists independent of the existence of the body. We need only identify increasingly with the soul's manifestations such as joy, peace, love, wisdom, and calmness in order to move step-by-step to a pure state of consciousness. Yogananda included in his definition of Self-realization that we need only "to improve our knowing." Or as modern authors representing the teaching of non-duality might put it: live in the *now!** Though many equate eternity as achieved only after the death of the body, this is a misunderstanding. It is the death of the ego, not the body, that opens the "Pearly Gates." Jesus put it very well, "the kingdom of heaven is within you."†

The concept that in the afterlife our physical body returns to us, re-laundered, so to speak, is understandable from the point of view of the ego but makes no sense from the point of view of the soul which needs no physical body to exist. To be made in the image of God is to be one with the consciousness of God. That consciousness requires no form and is bliss eternal.

There are some who, not wishing to describe that which is beyond description, adopt a form of stoicism: silent acceptance in the face of present-tense reality. I call it "chop wood and carry water" consciousness. Zen is one example of this approach. As honest and peaceful as this approach may be, its refusal to offer either solace or hope for "salvation" or "bliss" or any other form of ultimate fulfillment leaves some of us out in the cold, even if there are some who find comfort sitting in the present moment, alone.

* See books and talks by Eckhart Tolle.
† Luke 17:21

Does ridding oneself of desire include the desire for soul-fulfillment? Some say that it does. But robbed of the desire for Self-realization how can we achieve it? Others say we must cling to this one desire at the exclusion of all others in order to reach the desireless state before the fulfillment can arrive. *Sanatan Dharma* prefers the latter. After all, who would make the sacrifices required to obtain the "pearl of great price" without some expectation? A saying in India puts the paradox in a simple form: use a thorn to remove a thorn. If you narrow your desires to the one desire to know God (or be free, or however you want to put it) then you leverage an aspect of our dilemma which is the built-in tendency to "grasp" or "get." Such questions are forever debated among teachers, but rather than get stuck in words we can use whatever legitimate means, techniques, teachings, or practices we are offered to make the illusive and illusory thing called "progress." For it has been said that God is as much with us now as God will ever be. We need only to "improve our knowing" (our realization).

To again misquote the sage on the stage, Forrest Gump: "Heaven is as heaven does." Only that which truly fulfills the deep longing of our souls can be called heaven. Whatever draws us most swiftly and surely toward God is our raft over the ocean of delusion. As Yogananda wrote in a poem, "Let me be Christian, Jew, Hindu, Buddhist, Mohammedan, or Sufi: I care not what my religion, my race, my creed, or my color be, if only I can win my way to Thee!"

Chapter 22

Thou Shalt Not Have
False Gods

THE FIRST TWO OF THE TEN COMMANDMENTS ARE injunctions against the worship of false gods — gods other than the one God. Included is an injunction against the creation and worship of idols.*

Despite the innumerable gods and goddesses of Hinduism, *Sanatan Dharma* is, in its essence, monotheistic.† Even the most superficial study of the Vedas or the Bhagavad Gita or any number of other texts of India will reveal this truth.

In the ancient and highly nuanced culture of India, the gods and goddesses are agents of the One, just as you and I, and the creation itself, are manifestations of the One. Each god or goddess represents certain qualities or virtues of God as manifested in human lives. When Jesus declared himself one with the Father, he was accused of blasphemy. His response, however, was to quote back to his accusers their own scripture (the Old Testament) saying "Do not your scriptures say, 'Ye are gods?'"‡

---

* Exodus 20:3–5

† I am slightly tempted to give a long list of Hindu gods and goddesses and which qualities of divinity they symbolize but entire books have been written on this and I don't pretend to be a Hindu scholar.

‡ John 10:34 quoting Psalm 82:6

Judaism and Christianity (and Islam and other faiths) acknowledge the existence of angels, demons, and other disincarnate entities. I'm not sure if the title given (whether gods or angels) is that important.

The proscription against idols and false gods is directed toward the worship of lesser gods than the one God. But shouldn't it also be interpreted to include the "false gods" of name, fame, wealth, pleasure, and power? To these false gods, most people offer innumerable precious gifts of worship. The Bible tells the story of the golden calf worshipped by the Israelites in the Sinai desert. Did they really think they were worshipping an image of a calf in gold as if it were a god? I suspect that the "golden calf" was a metaphor for saying that the Israelites fell back into the worship of "gold" and everything it represents: money, pleasure, pride, and status.

I admit that the literal words of the commandment are such that a good Christian, Jew, or Muslim must shudder seeing all those "idols" in Hindu temples. And the Hindus make things worse by using the English word "idol" to describe them. Little do they know, having received the term innocently from their former British overlords, how shocking it seems to the Abrahamic faithful.

But they know perfectly well that no statue is God. Don't forget that Catholics have their crucifix and their statues too. In both Hinduism and in Catholicism there are veracious accounts of statues crying or bleeding or otherwise seeming to come to life! God exists in all things and perhaps especially in those symbols that are worshipped as containing the divine presence.

Swami Kriyananda put it this way: "I prefer to use the term 'ideals' rather than 'idols.'"

Chapter 23

Which Is Better: Prayer or Service?

THE FAMOUS MARTHA AND MARY STORY OF THE BIBLE only appears in the gospel of Luke.* They are commonly believed to be the sisters of Lazarus whom Jesus raised from the dead.

In that story Martha has the temerity to complain and even scold Jesus, insisting that Jesus tell her sister Mary to get up off the floor to help her, Martha, in the kitchen. Mary had been sitting before Jesus listening to him and absorbing his vibrations. Jesus was giving what Hindus and yogis call a *satsang*: a spiritual discourse. As is the case throughout the world when a spiritual teacher visits homes for this purpose, a meal is prepared. It evidently was the case that Martha ended up being the one to cook and feed Jesus and his flock of disciples.

Down through the centuries the debate has ebbed and flowed as to whether Martha was right, or Mary was right. I don't know why there was any debate because Luke quotes

* Luke 10:38–42

Jesus clearly as saying "Mary has chosen the better part." Did
Jesus mean to say that the contemplative life is always the
"better part"?

Other debates derived from trying to understand the implications of this story are framed in the context of asking
which of these are more spiritual: those who have a religious
vocation, or those who are householder-lay members of the
church? Or could it be between religious vocations in humanitarian service such as schools or hospitals versus those
who are cloistered in prayer?

One solution was offered to us long ago by Meister
Eckhart, a thirteenth century mystic. He taught that Martha
and Mary were really two sides of the same coin.* He knew
well the value of silence and contemplation but knew also
that the spiritual path does not exclude the performance of
our God-given and karma-given obligations. Paramhansa
Yogananda held the same view: prayer and service are both
necessary and integral to the spiritual life.

Yogananda represents an ancient tradition, the core practice of which is meditation. In this view meditation energizes
service because the experience of silence (as the presence of
God) enables one to act without selfish motive and as an act
of devotion. Meditation is the "better part" when it is understood that it helps us to serve more purely. At the same
time, meditation alone is not enough for all but the most
highly advanced souls: those who can meditate deeply all the
time. Selfless service is also purifying, and it energizes the
focus and the devotion of meditation. They go hand in hand.
Yogananda complained that too many of the wandering

---

* "Being at Home in Two Worlds: Meister Eckhart on Mary and Martha and the
Integration of the Active and Contemplative Life" Christopher Malcolm Knauf
blog, May 21, 2016.

"*sadhus*" in India were hardly better than bums begging for food from the householders (whom they disdained as weak), arguing amongst themselves, and neither meditating deeply nor performing selfless service. Meditation without service can strengthen the ego and make one lazy. Service without meditation will generate restlessness and attachment to outcomes.

Yogananda said he was sent to the West to resurrect the practice of "inner communion," that is: meditation as a form of prayer. He said, "Prayer is talking to God. Meditation is listening for God's response." It is the proverbial both-and truth. Both are needed, yet meditation is the foundation, and meditation goes together with service.*

---

* It has been said in India that a famous rishi, King Janaka, achieved Self-realization through service alone but while this sounds good, tradition has it that Janaka was *already* Self-realized before he was born.

Chapter 24

Saints and Theologians

ARLIER I QUOTED SWAMI KRIYANANDA AS QUOTING
Paramhansa Yogananda saying that "the saints are the
true custodians of religion." Yogananda quite possibly
also coined the term "Churchianity," which was his term for
distinguishing between religion and spirituality. The history
of Christianity reveals that the popes, clergy, religious orders,
and theologians sipped a chalice full of sanctity but also filled
barrels with sin, error, and debasement. Notwithstanding
self-serving statements of infallibility, authority, or spiritual power, millions of Christians have rejected the hierarchy
of Catholicism. In the initial stages of their "protest-rant"
movement, there was violence and warfare. But the seed of
the movement was to seek individual spiritual authenticity.
Looking back, it seems this has been a necessary step, though
the results thus far seem mixed at best.

As Mahatma Gandhi and later Rev. Martin Luther King,
Jr. put it, those in power do not surrender their position willingly. The growing number of people letting go of mainline
church affiliation or participation and becoming "spiritual
but not religious" is indicative of this ongoing protestation.

At its heart is a powerful impulse for seeking truth, however it is far easier to reject an old form in favor of a new one than it is to seek the truth underlying form all together.

This is being written during a worldwide pandemic and amidst ongoing polarization of opinions on society, science, economics, religion, and politics. Headlines tell us that distrust of authority is at an all-time high. As a child of the Sixties in the Bay Area of California, I have already "been there and done that" decades ago. But we must remember that there are millions who still go by the "old-time religion." My own brother is a Latin-rite Catholic priest whose views lie in the long shadow of the Holy Inquisition.

But the silently turning wheels of evolving consciousness are moving towards universality. Some authority is needed, however, lest chaos and anarchy reign supreme. This is true in society, politics, the professions, education, and industry as well as in matters of spiritual truth. Human values and virtue are unassailably conservative because kindness, compassion, and virtues like truth-telling are universal and timeless. In practice, such values are necessarily relative to the times, circumstances and social norms, but they are always sought and valued by those of goodwill and refinement.

Theologians and scholars make a worthy contribution to human understanding, but it is the saints who, in divine attunement, are the true disciples.* It is they, not the clerics

* What is a saint? A theologian? I do not know any useful definition of a saint but I'll offer that in my own usage I refer to one who has had direct and consistent experience of God. Evidence of this is traditionally considered to take the form of miracles. In the yoga tradition, repeated experiences of cosmic consciousness are evidenced by miraculous happenings and powers. As to theologians, well, I guess you get a college degree and then a job researching and publishing dogmas, church history, and related traditions. In India, I suppose a "pundit" is a form of theologian. Sometimes, though not usually, a saint can be a theologian and a theologian can be a saint. ("Both-And")

or even popes, who have greater and clearer access to divine guidance. However not every saint is equally attuned, nor does every saint have a divinely given role to play in the guidance of any body of worshippers. Sometimes we don't really appreciate or understand a saint's message until the saint is long dead.* Yet history attests to their uplifting influence and example.

Even a cursory examination of religious institutions reveals that the relationship between leadership and sanctity is, at best, tenuous. Large, complicated modern institutions will tend to draw able administrators not saints. Administrators are more likely to vote into office those who are more like themselves, rather than the saintly ones, for the obvious fact that you never know what a saintly soul is going to do or say next! (Or at least such is the common perception.) Nonetheless, there have been church leaders who were saintly. There have even been political leaders who were saintly.

I'm not suggesting a movement towards appointing saints to positions of authority in religious organizations. However, I am suggesting that individual devotees look to the saints for inspiration and guidance. Priests, monks, and nuns do good work (usually) but if there is a saint among them it is that person whose counsel or example we should look to. Let the hierarchy do their work to keep the "hive" running efficiently but it's the "honey" of divine consciousness that the real devotee-bees are seeking.

You may ask, and rightly so, "How do I know a saint when I see one?" Jesus' reply to that was "By their fruits you

* The Catholic Church has a curious role in the lives of saints: the church's well-known persecution of a living saint helps make the person a saint while its post-mortem beatification insures the saint's legacy!

shall know them."* The church has a strict regimen of miracles that a would-be saint must pass (safely, after their death)
but the lay population ferrets out the miracles long before
any church notices. This is of course a personal and complex
matter and people can be mistaken. I recommend reading
the lives of the saints, and because the need in our times is
for ego transcendence and transcendent perceptions, look
to the mystics for true guidance. In Christianity, some who
offer enormous wisdom and devotion include St. Francis,
St. Teresa of Avila, St. John of the Cross, St. Anthony of the
Desert, Padre Pio, and Therese Neumann.

Not everyone is ready for or interested in saints. For most
church goers, the church they attend serves their spiritual
aspirations even as they, in turn, help others with whom
they associate. The goal of higher consciousness means they
seek to be better people and do good in the world. Of course,
there are some who attend out of habit, fear of God, or fear
of criticism, or simply to maintain their social status. The
goal of union with God is not even imagined and presumably
never suggested. Fortunately, spiritually speaking, God offers wisdom and solace at every level of spiritual motivation
and consciousness.

* Matt 7:20

Chapter 25

Morals: Absolute or Relative?

I N THE FIRST HALF OF THE TWENTIETH CENTURY, during the lifetime of Paramhansa Yogananda, some of the issues debated included war, colonialism, economic exploitation, rising rates of divorce, and materialism. While he had specific views on many issues, his view was conservative and emphasized moderation, loyalty, compassion, generosity, and justice. Yogananda offered advice on improving diet (emphasizing vegetarianism) and wrote how-to-live tracts on success, marriage, parenting, and civic life. Swami Kriyananda, a disciple trained by Yogananda, explained that in private Yogananda had serious misgivings about the "New Deal" for its potential to erode private initiative and responsibility.* Yet he was also deeply passionate about the importance of helping others less fortunate than oneself.

What might Yogananda have said in response to the issues of the present time? Among these issues are the sex-gender ones of abortion, contraception, homosexuality,

---

* It is worth noting, I believe, that during the last decade or so of Yogananda's life, America and the West were in the grip of fear over the potential for communism (avowedly atheistic) to erode personal initiative and freedoms.

and transgender identities. More widely applicable are the issues of global warming, cloning, globalization, and artificial intelligence. Yogananda viewed what later came to be called "globalization" as a trend with the potential to connect people economically, socially, and politically. It could only be positive if it also fostered greater equality, respect, and cooperation.

On sexual matters, Yogananda was conservative and traditional. I suspect he would wonder what all the fuss was about on gay and transgender questions. He accepted people simply as he saw them: as souls, not bodies, or personalities. He surely would not endorse violence or discrimination. He actively fought against the racism of his time. Being dark-skinned himself, he was thoroughly acquainted with it.

And finally, on matters of ecology, Yogananda was concerned about the impact of humanity's treatment of the earth and its natural resources. His remarks implied that he foresaw coming natural disasters triggered by negative attitudes and behavior.

Timeless truths are both conservative and progressive. The law of karma is an example of the conservative side of spirituality as illustrated by Jesus' statement "The poor ye shall have always with you."* Justice is the result of personal merit while mercy comes from grace, from compassion.† Politics, like life itself, lurches from conservative to progressive and back again according to the situation at hand. Each contains potentially valid points of view.

But the time-tested values of the saints have never wavered from urging moderation, self-control, loyalty, and ego

* Matt 27:11
† "…Verily I say unto you, inasmuch as ye have done it unto one of the least of these my brethren, ye have done it unto me." — Matt 25:34–40

transcendence. Pleasure (and pain) are part of life and therefore have their legitimate place in the human experience.
God and the soul are supersensory and transcendent, and it
is to this realm of consciousness that the saints and *avatars*
direct our attention. We are seeing the end of an epoch and
the beginning of a new age of understanding. The change
requires old forms, institutions, lifestyles, and dogmas to
make way for a new understanding, even of eternal and unchanging truths. The dissolution of old forms and beliefs can
appear to destroy traditional values, but the destruction, like
a winter storm, can prepare the soil of human consciousness
for renewed growth. The expectation Yogananda shared is
that humanity, after a time of chaos and disintegration, will
recenter its values in true and lasting truths.

Chapter 26

Faith, Belief, and Intuition

BELIEF APPLIED ENERGETICALLY BUT SENSITIVELY to one's life can gradually become faith if anchored in truth. St. Paul states "Now faith is the substance of things hoped for, the evidence of things unseen."* Faith consists of the conviction that the goodness of Providence shall prevail, notwithstanding present, outward appearances. The strength of conviction is its "substance" and this includes the calm certitude of inner knowing. Belief might also be for "things hoped for," but belief lacks the conviction that faith, which is tested belief, bestows. This conviction or inner knowing is another way of describing intuition which is the "sixth sense" that reveals what cannot otherwise be known through reason or the senses. Faith and intuition are inextricably linked and are virtually interchangeable — though not in our common linguistic usage. A person's firm conviction is "evidence" of that faith but it is also a reference to the demonstrated result of that person's faith, whether in a specific circumstance or as shown repeatedly in that person's life.

* Hebrews 11:1

"Credo!" "I believe!" How many arguments, books, and wars have been fought over "credo." I listened to a recording of Christian church history that told of a dispute between Chalcedons and non-Chalcedons in the fourth century A.D. in which ten thousand people were killed in Alexandria, Egypt over beliefs about Jesus's divine nature!* It's truly staggering how far from "turn the other cheek" Christians and other religionists have strayed. Paramhansa Yogananda had a phrase he used: "Fools argue, the wise discuss."

Belief is like a scientific hypothesis: only experimentation can produce the evidence to turn belief into the intuitive knowing of faith. Faith comes from the descent of grace triggered by the right effort to tune into the "truth that shall make us free." Faith does not necessarily reveal advance knowledge of the outcome, though this might be included, but it rests upon the inner certitude that God is the Doer and no matter what may come, it must be spiritually right for our soul's evolution. Faith is trust in God. When St. Paul says "things hoped for" he's not talking about a lovely home or an expensive car. What is hoped for is for divine grace to guide us through the storms and trials of life. The intuitive feeling of true faith is, to us at least, the evidence of the unseen guidance of God.

Belief has its place as a starting point in making practical the steps along our spiritual journey. When, as we advance along the path, our belief matures into faith and we live increasingly by God's grace, we find protection and divine guidance along the way. Prayer is a classic

* Not surprisingly the dispute was more political than theological but its basis was the definition of the true nature of Jesus Christ: divine and/or human.

example of how belief can be transformed into faith. I'm not talking about the typical prayer for material things, comfort, or even health. Rather, it is the practice of sharing with God our thoughts, and praying to God for the grace to know, love, and serve Him. Our daily practice, if sincere and focused, will typically yield the "evidence" of increased calmness, quiet inner joy, devotion, and the gift of intuition (knowing what to do or say in the moment of our need).

By contrast, if our belief in the providence of God is focused on what we *want* from God, it will inevitably turn to presumption, and we will probably become disillusioned. At first the difference is subtle because it is not unusual that prayers for material benefits may yield results; but the longer-term effects are not subtle. These longer-term effects include the potential for pride in concluding: "I am special because God answers my prayers." Pride will lead to frustration and anger when the benefits trickle to a stop owing to our very pride. Pride, you see, precedes the fall from the flow of grace. When we are accepting of what God gives us in life, then there can be no question of presumption. If what comes or doesn't come shatters our expectations, then it wasn't faith, it was only hope. It was probably a desire for specific results. This kind of hope differs from St. Paul's reference to "hope" because St. Paul's hope is rooted in humility and offered in surrender.

Paramhansa Yogananda wrote that "Intuition is the soul's power to know God." He also taught that meditation is the most effective means by which we can develop and deepen our intuitional ability, called the "sixth sense." (To "know God" includes knowing those things our personal circumstances require.) In meditation, intuition is best developed after meditation techniques are finished and the meditator sits in silent inner communion with God or one of the manifested aspects of God such as peace, light, sound, love, power, joy, energy, or calmness. I am not aware of any teachings in Christianity comparable to this other than the actual experiences of the mystics.

When Jesus replied to Peter that "upon this rock I will build my church," Yogananda taught that Jesus was referring to Peter's intuition as the rock.* I have read that the interpretation of this famous statement is hotly debated between Catholics and Protestants. Catholic interpretation is that Peter is the rock, and the Catholic church and its succession of popes, are what Jesus' power and teachings are built upon. Protestants claim that the recognition of Jesus as the Messiah, the son of God, is the rock upon which the church of Christ is built. Admittedly, "Petros" in Latin means "rock," so Jesus was giving Simon Bar-Jonah a new name and that it is upon Peter that this "church" is to be built! No matter how one interprets the words of Jesus, Peter clearly was given spiritual sight by which he had "eyes to see" what others, including the other disciples present, did not see — or at least could not attest to with such power and clarity as Peter.

But for you and me, it is upon intuition — the unshakeable rock, or foundation, of higher consciousness — that the "church" of our growing faith towards cosmic consciousness is built. Intuition and faith bestow an inner certitude that gives one insight, whereas others might only affirm belief. Whether Jesus intended the word "church" to refer to the

* Matt 16:15–19

organization of believers or, as Yogananda taught, the wisdom of the soul, both interpretations fit. The former belongs to church history while the latter belongs to every aspiring soul. When Peter identified Jesus as the Messiah, Jesus' comment was that it was not reason, the senses, or public opinion that revealed his identity to Peter; it was intuition.

In Western culture, intuition is not well understood. We admit that sometimes we have had a hunch that proved true, and there are well-known examples, such as the theory of relativity coming to Einstein in a flash, or famous classical composers receiving entire symphonies into their minds; but our culture isn't oriented to recognize these as anything other than random phenomena "out of the blue."

Ironically, research has repeatedly proven the existence of telepathy as a form of communication which requires no medium of transmission and is not diminished by distance or time. Yet, being inexplicable to our reason, we simply shrug our proverbial shoulders.

In the East, however, the awareness and acceptance of intuition is embedded into the culture. In former times, a Westerner might have been approached on the street by a Hindu psychic and, without invitation, been told his fortune! While the image of Hindu fortune-tellers is grist for the mill of stereotypical depiction, it does illustrate the pervasive role that intuition plays in the culture. Other cultures might be especially notable for their belief in magic or psychic phenomenon.

Mystics of East and West attest to having visions of Jesus or other great masters, or of being visited by an angel who brings a message. These angelic messengers are seen in the New Testament as the angels that appeared to Mary, Joseph, and Zachariah.

In the West we are not taught, nor therefore do we possess, an expectation that we can consciously develop our intuitional abilities, yet our "sixth sense" is the gateway to success, ideas, inspiration, and ultimately, to higher realms of reality and consciousness. After all, of the many psychics on "hotlines," surely there must be one or two who truly *are* psychic! Although we "use" it, or more correctly, intuition "feeds" us ideas, solutions and inspiration, we don't reflect upon what it is and how it works.

When Jesus responded to Peter's declaration that Jesus was the Messiah and pronounced that he, Peter, would be given the "keys," Yogananda interpreted that the "keys" represented access to these higher realms via intuition. Meditation, Yogananda taught, holds the "key" to the intuitional realm because by regular meditation, properly practiced and understood, we can develop the muscle of the "sixth sense." In the ultimate sense, true divine guidance comes from within, not from a pope or a church. Enlightened beings, not prelates, forgive sins, heal the sick, raise the dead and bring to humanity the promise of our soul's immortality.*

Can intuition, the key to higher knowledge, be obtained by willpower alone? Can access to the key be sought by pounding on the door of the psyche; or does one need a guru, a savior, to hand it over? In other words,

---

* This doesn't deny the value of having an organization, or the need for some form of authority and processes of decision making. But spiritual truth comes from revelation, and revelation is channeled through the inner experience of intuition. Of course, not just anyone's claim of intuition is to be believed. One must have demonstrated sanctity and attunement.

does intuition come by effort or by grace? The eternal question with the eternal response: yes, and no. Or, as I prefer: "Both-And."

The yogis say intuition *can* be developed by daily and ever deeper meditation. A saint or an *avatar* can even bestow the power of intuition upon a disciple. For example, Swami Kriyananda tells the story of his early days as a young twenty-two-year-old monk who suddenly was raised to the position of head monk. As such he interviewed prospective monks for acceptance into the monastery. Evidently, he had one or two instances where his judgement was less than "spot-on." Yogananda, his guru, told him, "I'm going to have to give you intuition!" After that, he had no further problems with identifying men suitable to be accepted as monks.

Yogananda was once getting ready for a lecture and a reporter-interviewer asked him the question: "Can inspiration be put under the command of will?" Though busy with his preparations, he stopped and replied: "Yes. Take down this poem." In that moment, he spontaneously dictated a new poem which was later included in his book *Whispers from Eternity*. After the publication of the book, a well-known literary critic selected that very same poem as an example of one of Yogananda's best prayer-poems.

Intuition and faith are, so far as I can understand them, related. Yogananda's faith (his intuitive knowing) was the source for his saying "Yes. Take down this poem." Faith produced the inner certitude that he could demonstrate what he claimed, but intuition gave him the poem. While an accomplished composer, scientist, politician, or parent might be an intuitive person in their field of expertise, the devotee develops faith in God as the window through which divine guidance (aka intuition) comes.

Although this book is not about meditation, it is worth noting that there is an important connection between meditation and intuition. Faith blossoms in calmness, humility, and openness and increases one's receptivity to intuition. Meditation deepens when the ego-self is becalmed and receptive. They go hand in hand. As I mentioned earlier, Yogananda counseled that to increase access to intuition one should sit calmly after the practice of one's chosen meditation technique. This receptivity gradually and increasingly permeates one's waking hours and even dreams. Thus, meditation becomes one of the most effective means to develop intuitive powers.

Testing Intuition

I cannot complete this chapter without a fair warning: You must test your intuition. Consider those self-proclaimed gurus who predicted the end of the world. Upon what intuition did they declare their knowing? John the Evangelist counsels us to "test the spirits." * Similarly, consider Jesus' statement "Be wise as serpents and harmless as doves."† Intuition is not impressed by brash demands. We mustn't imagine that the sphere of intuition is a blind, dumb force. Far from it.

One reason intuition is held in suspicion by the reasoning faculty is that it can seem fickle. Indeed, intuition is on the emotional spectrum, though it lies at the calmer, feeling end (as opposed to the wild and uncontrollable emotional end).

* 1 John 4:1
† Matt 10:16

Intuition often announces itself through the faculty of feeling and can come in a variety of forms such as images, words of instruction, commands or suggestions, or it might appear as a fully formed impression of a potential future reality.

If intuition defies common sense, universal spiritual and human values, and the specific counsel of one's spiritual teacher, be more than cautious! Swami Kriyananda wrote an excellent book on how to develop and test intuition, so I will only offer a few points here. First, always remember that true intuition is calm, confident, and knowing. If your response is excitement or any other emotional state, be on your guard. Also, if following your intuition might expose you to criticism or require heroic efforts, let the calm sense of rightness be your guide. But do not fall into the New Age excuse for passivity that says: If it is meant to be, it will be. Rather have the attitude: If it is the right thing, I must make the effort. Lastly, do not plunge headlong into following your inner guidance. Keep your intuition radar alert for additional guidance that might alter your steps or direction at any time.

Is Intuition Effort or Grace?

Christianity meets *Sanatan Dharma* at the fulcrum point of intuition because openness to divine guidance requires willpower, while the guidance itself constitutes grace. Intuition functions like a "worm hole" or portal into a higher realm. Only when we begin to appreciate the opportunity of intuition can we discover the source of universal consciousness that is available to all souls equally. Prayer and meditation are a way of attuning our hearts and minds to the field of knowing, of grace, of guidance, and of intuition. But while prayer is talking, meditation is listening for a response. The Bible says, "Be still and *know!*"* We should approach this "knowing" with reverence and humility, because this realm is not a function of ego.

On the other hand, Paramhansa Yogananda is known for an entire collection of what he termed "Prayer-Demands," in which he suggests that we pray not as a beggar but as a son (or daughter). The "demand" he speaks of is not from the ego, it is a modern version of Jesus' counsel that we should "pray believing." This means that we should pray with calm confidence in our Father-Mother's desire to bestow that which is best for us.†

Yogananda termed the higher state of awareness from which intuition comes as "superconsciousness." Other terms exist and approximate in varying degrees the same idea: the Collective Unconscious, Panpsychism, the Akashic field, and many more. As a life-long meditator I live with the faith that what I need to know will appear when I need it. This is not a boast, and thus the statement must be offered humbly and tentatively ("that which is hoped for"). I can think of no more satisfying way to live a life which brings us never ending surprises, twists, turns, challenges, and opportunities.

My spiritual guide, Swami Kriyananda, was extraordinary in both the quality and quantity of his creativity, inspiration, and energy. He wrote hundreds of pieces of music, well over one hundred books, founded communities, gave thousands of talks, made countless videos, gave untold number of personal interviews, and he did all of

* Psalm 46:10
† Matt 21:22

this in the face of opposition, even persecution, as well as many medical challenges.

Intuition: A Higher State of Energy

I haven't yet mentioned one important ingredient of true intuition: energy. The superconscious state is one of higher vibration and energy level. A bored, tired, selfish, or sense-addicted person is not as likely to have ready access to intuition as is a person who considers the needs of others, serves the cause of high ideals, and prays and meditates daily. Of course, as with all talents, creativity can be used for good or ill. Even criminals can express creative genius in their career. Indeed, some of the world's most evil people have been people of tremendous energy and willpower. My point is that intuition is not a function of passivity.

Intuition is the key to the evolution of Christianity in that, when understood rightly, it can reopen the door to what had formerly been decried as obscurantism, superstition, miracles, or mystical experiences. The development of our sixth sense faculty should be approached with the right attitude and by using a scientific method (meditation). Its findings should be held up tentatively to the test of reason and commonsense. Christians who seek direct perception of the divine will and presence can experience the soul's innate divinity. Nothing could be more revolutionary and healing than this.

Great scientists, artists, and leaders already avail themselves of intuitive guidance, but our culture is not aware of how to develop and trust inner guidance. Only a few, on the fringe of our confused society, have done so to date. It is time for spiritual seekers, too, to gain access to "the truth that shall make us free."*

In the Yoga Sutras of Patanjali, the signs of spiritual progress are given and are known as the *siddhis*. These are familiar to Christians as the power of mystics to levitate, walk on water or fire, bi-locate, to use clairvoyance, clairaudience, telepathy, and much more. All such powers derive from the devotee's commitment to achieving transcendent states of mind beyond thought. However, seekers are warned from coveting such powers for their own sake just as devotees are warned from indulging in sense-delights for the sake of pleasure alone.

Only the seeker with a pure heart can receive such powers and not fall from grace by their misuse. But what else is God if not the holder and giver of all power? Swami Kriyananda commented that material gifts like name, fame, wealth, and pleasure can never last and are always on the verge of being lost or stolen, but soul-powers are our very nature and are thus true. Such powers have no self-regulating opposites other than our misuse of them.

The superconscious intuitive state of the soul is the bridge between human and divine consciousness. With self-effort we can learn to be more intuitive and more humanly creative, but our effort alone is not sufficient to lead us permanently to the promised land. For that, the soul needs its "Moses," a true guru. We have already covered this topic.

Of course, being innately children of the Infinite, all people live to some degree by this power. But those who draw on it and use it merely for ego gratification will rise and fall according to the law of karma.

* John 8:32

Belief then is where we begin our spiritual adventure. As we make sincere and energetic efforts to live by the spiritual precepts that we have embraced, we draw the grace that lifts us upward toward the realm of intuition whereby we become "seers." Seeing the higher truths that guide our lives, we develop the faith and conviction to live ever more certainly by truth and inner guidance.

Chapter 27

Is Creativity of the Ego or of the Soul?

Is Ego Transcendence Contractive or Expansive?

INTUITION IS NECESSARILY CREATIVE BECAUSE WE ARE opening ourselves to guidance that we, in our conscious mind or by our subconscious inclinations, would not have accessed. Being creative is fun; creativity inspires enthusiasm! Creativity is self-expansive though it can challenge our energy, our self-definitions, and even our courage to act on the intuition received.

Traditional religious attitudes and practices seek to get rid of the ego. Keeping one's head down is encouraged and, if one is a monk or nun, it also makes life easier for the superiors. Ego transcendence is, from this point of view, a contractive and not an expansive process. The last thing religious superiors want to deal with is a bunch of enthusiastic monastics bursting with new ideas. But whether one is in a religious order or is a devout and humble householder, the same expectation of "head down" has prevailed. "Carry your cross" and "don't complain" is, or was, the expectation. In an environment where creativity is viewed with the suspicion that it is coming from and affirming the ego, it is safer not to risk critique by expressing it.*

Overcoming egotism has valid spiritual virtue. Christianity's emphasis on dissolution of the ego has not prevented saints of great spiritual stature from arising. But does ego bashing and carrying one's cross with head down generate inspiration in the twenty-first century? I don't mean to suggest that Jesus' crucifixion is no longer a source of gratitude and inspiration to Christians. But I wonder to what extent sincere Christians find themselves inspired to imitate Jesus' response to the injustice of his trial, torture, and crucifixion? Would we watch mutely if this were to happen today? While we admire Jesus' acceptance of the will of this Father, the consciousness of our times is an inclination to ask questions and want to know more about the details and consequences.

Paramhansa Yogananda, as an individual and as a teacher, expressed and encouraged creativity and enthusiasm. He demonstrated that striving to overcome the ego was the funeral of sorrows, not a sorrow-filled funeral. Why? Because breaking the narrow bounds of egoity brings freedom, and freedom brings joy!

If you study more closely the lives of the Christian saints, you will see they were fountainheads of originality and enthusiasm. St. Francis, for example, was the first to write poetry in his own language (rather than Latin). He invented a technique of making stone archways and ceilings. He was the

---

* A similar "via negativa" existed in Eastern spirituality during the last two millennia.

first to recreate the nativity scene of Jesus' birth. An aphorism of the medieval period was that "a sad saint is a sad saint indeed."* Even though Jesus has been described as a "man of sorrows," how could thousands have flocked to hear him speak if he were only going to wag a disapproving finger at them with a long face?

Nonetheless, there is no denying that the historical emphasis in Christianity on sorrow and suffering was, in the past, the hallmark of spiritual life. For us now, spiritual growth is characterized by calm acceptance and inner joy. There is a revival of a joyful spirituality taking place in our times. To understand this, however, we should take a detour to examine the dichotomy between modern consciousness and medieval attitudes.

We Are at a Spiritual Crossroads

Yogananda approved of the cheerful optimism of the American spirit. America was founded on the search for personal liberty. Freedom of action has unlocked an avalanche of creativity, not just in America but worldwide. The consciousness of the human right for freedom of choice continues to grow. One cannot deny, however, that unrestrained personal liberties have the potential to become chaotic, exploitative, and selfish. Commonsense alone tells us that personal freedom has a concomitant virtue: personal responsibility.

Spirituality is at a crossroads. Commonsense is far from sufficient to guide young adults into a balanced, healthy, and responsible life. Rules and dogmas have steadily lost their power to share traditional values. Erecting billboards with

---

* "A sad saint is a sad saint, indeed" (St. Francis de Sales); and, "A sad nun is a bad nun." (St. Teresa of Avila)

the Ten Commandments doesn't seem to have much impact, nor does shouting "Thou shalt *not!*" Orthodox religion has been railing against modern trends in lifestyles and behavior for several centuries, but it is losing ground.

Might the creative Creator have another solution in mind? Maybe the fact that Christians don't seem particularly inspired to turn "the other cheek" suggests that God, through our own intuition, is guiding us in another direction. I'm not suggesting we seek revenge as an alternative, but there might be other responses to injury, abuse, condemnation, and violence than forbearance.

Freedom, Yes, but for All

The modern era has been characterized by the urge for freedom from externally imposed social, religious, racial, and economic forms of repression, exploitation, abuse, and prejudice. Some of the greatest reformers in modern times have been spiritual crusaders for justice.* Jesus himself drove the moneychangers from the temple precincts. Serfdom, slavery, trafficking, sweat shops, child labor—on and on in our times has rolled the juggernaut of freedom from oppression. Paramhansa Yogananda was not alone in identifying the two world wars as catalysts for the destruction of colonialism and the freedom of oppressed Asian and African peoples from Western powers.

A powerful and creative upwelling has been underway since about the time of the Renaissance. It is far from over. The Catholic Church, especially, and other Christian sects to some degree, have attempted to stifle this urge for freedom.

* Mahatma Gandhi; Rev. Martin Luther King, Jr.; Nelson Mandela.

Sadly, most Christian churches seem to have sided with the established and hierarchical governmental institutions of their respective times.* Must Christians consider this tidal wave something of the devil? If so the American revolution, Mahatma Gandhi, Rev. Martin Luther King, Jr., and Nelson Mandela are instruments of Satan.

The freedoms won in America and other countries have triggered an enormous amount of creative energy in science, business, engineering, and the arts. This tsunami of creativity has, even if only from a material point of view, helped millions to achieve greater financial security and greater awareness and acceptance of diversity through education, travel, and communication. Of course, a sizeable percentage of these activities feed only people's materialistic urges, but like the adolescent let loose into early adulthood, sometimes you must discover for yourself what works and what doesn't.

Our urge for freedom of choice has its source in the Creator's choice to manifest the creation. As described in an earlier chapter, we too are endowed with the urge to create and have been given the choice to seek our happiness either in the material world or in the consciousness of Spirit, the Creator.

The inclination of modern consciousness is toward expansion of self-identity and awareness, and, toward personal freedom. Passive acceptance of our lot in life as God's will is no longer the ticket price of spiritual growth. We admire stories of "rags to riches" success for these suggest energy, pluckiness, and creativity.

* Many have noted that the monarchial view of creation, with God above on his throne and Jesus on his right, clashes with the modern trend of egalitarianism and democracy (even in their imperfect manifestations).

What Was It Like Before?

To understand the direction of human consciousness we must go back in time and consider the fixed caste system of medieval times (East and West). With no choices, forbearance was the necessary and right attitude both practically and spiritually. My Irish mother would say to me as a child when I would complain: "Offer it up to Jesus, son!" This approach is perfectly valid, especially with those circumstances that one can do little about, such as a grumpy coworker or neighbor, a stubbed toe, or a death sentence from disease or old age.

Nonetheless, we live in culture where we have come to expect choices and we feel we have a right to be respected and to express ourselves freely in our pursuit, as we Americans say, of "happiness." A monk might understandably scoff and call this egotism, and of course, to a degree it is. But the more important question is whether this new self-identity can be spiritualized. Consider the opposite question: Can anyone become a saint with a negative self-image and a lack of confidence?

When I was growing up in the 1950s and 1960s surrounded by local priests and nuns, I considered becoming a priest. However, as I grew older, I observed a veritable tidal wave of priests and nuns leaving their religious vocations. I later learned that during those same years monasteries around the world were emptied of perhaps millions of former monks and nuns. Some were forced out by communist regimes, but many in Europe and America and Asia left by choice. Assuming that most were sincere in their original religious calling, I think many simply did not find a suitable environment to express their ideals.

As mentioned above, traditional medieval monasticism did not encourage being creative, enthusiastic, and joyful. In the 1950s (when I was a boy), strict obedience to one's parents, teachers, and adults was generally the norm both at work and at home. Punishment was swift and tactile.

Yogananda used the term "A New Dispensation" to describe a reversal of the attitude of ego suppression in favor of self-expression, self-respect, enthusiasm, and creativity.* It by no means eclipses universal virtues such as humility and devotion but this new emphasis redirects our spiritual aspirations towards a more expansive and inclusive direction.

To his close disciples, Yogananda gave direct counsel on the importance and the means to overcome the ego. But his counsel was not grim. It was imbued with confidence and energy. His public teaching, however, emphasized the positive. This wasn't hypocrisy on his part for several reasons: first, only those who came to him for discipline and guidance were asking for and accepting of the self-discipline required for ego transcendence; secondly, most who found his Eastern teachings fascinating, new, and novel were still at the exploration phase of the spiritual path he offered; and, lastly, two thousand years of emphasizing suffering is not something easily reversed. The birth of a new covenant or dispensation is like turning a great ship in the opposite direction. A strong positive affirmation is therefore needed.

Yogananda needed to address both ego transcendence and self-expansion as appropriate to best help those whom he served. We see this same distinction in the life of Jesus. When his disciples complained to him of his use of parables,

---

* Yogananda's use of this term is not limited to my one-sentence description of it. But in general it represents an expansion of consciousness and awareness as the hallmark of emerging spirituality.

Jesus explained that the parables were for the public but that he would speak plainly to them, his disciples.*

Wouldn't you say that putting your energy and attention in a positive direction is a more satisfying approach than fighting an old and undesirable one? There is a difference between suppression and sublimation. Sublimation is a form of behavioral modification. It is transformation from a negative behavior pattern to a new and more positive one. Positive directions are more energizing than fighting negative patterns.

If negative habits continue to plague us, we may need to confront them more directly.† But if our positive efforts to meditate, serve selflessly, pray, and express devotion to God are themselves sufficient to set a new course in life, then why even think about the past?

Self-expansion, in other words, is a characteristic of this new dispensation. There are two basic directions in spiritual growth: self-denial or self-expansion. We can destroy the ego or expand the ego toward Infinity.

Self-expansion is more likely to be creative than self-denial. Yogananda had a public ministry throughout his life and his secretaries could hardly keep up with him. He slept very little. Swami Kriyananda, too, traveled constantly, created courses, wrote music, wrote books, counseled, and corresponded until the very day of his death. Toward the end of his life, he commented "I no longer know where Kriyananda ends and Yogananda begins."

---

* Matt 13:10–16

† Unfortunately, some neophyte meditators try to overcome addictions or mental challenges only with meditation. Some, for example, cease the use of important medications in the expectation that only meditation is needed. While this is possible, meditation teachers are wise to send such students to their therapists or doctors for approval.

Throughout the history of Christianity, we have seen heroic levels of service in ordinary Christians and saints alike. The lives of the apostles are good examples. But as the centuries rolled forward, the image of the monk, priest, or nun tended to close in upon itself as a path principally characterized by self-denial. This was also true in Asia where seeking God or truth was characterized by extreme asceticism.

I don't want to leave the impression that working long hours in public ministry is what I mean by the path of Self-expansion. The essence of Self-expansion means including the realities of others with your own. It is self-forgetfulness in the love for God, even in the face of personal suffering. Ironically, too great an emphasis on suffering is potentially a form of self-involvement!

Humility: The Foundation for Spiritual Awakening

This positive approach to God must rest on a foundation of humility. True humility is positive — it is not self-abasement. True humility accepts our place in the grand scheme of creation and the sole reality behind it — the Creator. There is, therefore, only one kind of humility because as Yogananda put it: "Inferiority and superiority complexes are still of the ego." Instead, true humility is self-forgetfulness. The secret of humility as the basis for self-expansion is that while the ego may be inadequate to accomplish God's will, if I offer myself as an instrument of that will, God, through me, can accomplish anything. Even here, however, one must be careful not to let the clever ego step in to claim the credit!

Anyone performing their rightful duties with the right attitude — whether at home, at work or in a religious vocation — can do so with humility when humility is understood in this way. Anyone who is sincere can perform their duties cheerfully, as an act of devotion, and as a channel for divine blessings to others. In this spirit, creativity can blossom. As Swami Kriyananda put it: "It's not *what* you do, it's *how* you do it." By this he meant, the attitude with which you do something. This is what yogis call "karma yoga." In the Bhagavad Gita the term *nishkam karma* is used to describe the performance of duties without self-interest, personal reward, or desire for the results to accrue to oneself. In a more elevated way, *nishkam karma* can be expanded to mean that God is the doer working through you.

Joy Is the Fruit of Love for God

This new dispensation is beautifully depicted in the following lines of the poetic and musical Festival of Light ceremony which takes place at many of the Ananda temples on Sundays.

> . . . and whereas suffering and sorrow, in the past, were the coin of man's redemption, for us now the payment has been exchanged for calm acceptance and joy. Thus, may we understand that pain is the fruit of self-love, whereas joy is the fruit of love for God.

Rather than emphasizing the crucifixion of ego, we emphasize the expansion of joy that comes from offering the little self into the Great Light of God. Joy, not sorrow, becomes the hallmark of spiritual life. This has always been the case and can be seen when you study the lives of the saints, but it has not generally been depicted as such by ordinary Christians, priests, and ministers.

The furrowed-brow depiction is not entirely the fault of priests and clerics. The worldly person will always, in every age, view renunciation of personal desires with disdain and as a form of suffering. The worldly person, moreover, sees the spiritual life as an unhappy one.

Let me reiterate, however, that there remains a need for redirecting ego-affirming attitudes and habits.* The devotee will always need to keep a close watch on that clever ego.†

Energy and Creativity

A dull and lazy person cannot be a saint. Saints are people of power who apply creativity appropriately to their life's circumstances. This aspect of the new dispensation isn't new‡ but its emphasis is much needed in our times so that a greater number of people can be inspired to turn to God and reject the view of the spiritual life as one of deprivation, sorrow, and dullness.

Consider the great works of art and architecture throughout the world which, while costly and requiring great sacrifices, are wonders to behold. What energy! What creativity! What joy must have been experienced! Only devotion and dedication — not suffering — could have given birth to such monuments.

---

* Paramhansa Yogananda stated bluntly to Swami Kriyananda (then a young monk "whining" about his assigned duties) that "Living for God is martyrdom!" (For the ego, that is.)

† Can meditation be creative? Absolutely! By opening ourselves up to superconsciousness there is no end to the potential inspiration that can be offered to us. "Out of the silence came the song of creation" are the words from the music of the Festival of Light mentioned earlier. Meditation naturally produces a joyful and creative baseline attitude and self-expression. I could write another book on the difference between self-negating styles of meditation and self-expanding styles.

‡ Is anything born of Truth ever really "new"?

Back to Commonsense

I want, lastly, to go back to my statement that rules and dogmas are insufficient guides to the modern mind, especially the younger generations. I started with the concept of intuition, and I have already linked intuition with meditation. The deeper aspect of the change in human consciousness will come from the growing practice of meditation. The term "mindfulness" is the most used to describe the practice of meditation. Regardless of terms, the impact of meditation is greater awareness of one's own thoughts, feelings, and actions. Meditation helps a person to become more aware of the realities of others. This manifests first as awareness and later as sympathy, connection, and compassion. It has been said that if ten percent of the world's human population meditated every day, war, prejudice, abuse, and exploitation would rapidly disappear. Why? Because enough people would no longer feel in tune with corporate, governmental, or personal actions and attitudes that are harmful to others, including the natural world. Thus, our conscience is awakened and becomes our inner guide. The need for religious rules, already becoming increasingly ineffective, would diminish greatly.

Chapter 28

So, What Choice Do We Have?

THE AGE WE LIVE IN EMPHASIZES FREEDOM: FREEDOM of choice. We've covered that ground already. But a discussion of what constitutes the soul's free will is, like that of human sexuality in the twenty-first century, a difficult and unpopular one. For starters and to be clear, predestination has no voice in this discussion. Let me reiterate the idea that God started this whole thing by making a choice, based on a "desireless-desire." It is not surprising that we have also inherited a similar impulse.

Regardless of what anyone thinks about the extent of our human free will, the only choice we *haven't* been given is the fact of our creation to begin with. And according to both Genesis and the teachings of *Sanatan Dharma*, the first choice we, or if you prefer, our first parents, made was to separate ourselves from God so that we could find personal fulfillment in the creation itself.

It seems to us that we make choices every day. But why do we choose to wear one item in preference to another; or choose one dish for dinner instead of another; why do we find ourselves attracted to one person but repulsed by another; why we are drawn to one faith or to no faith; why were we born in this family and not some other? We really have no way to explain most of either our life circumstances or the choices we think we make. The law of karma, however, says these choices are the result of actions in past lives.*

But the most important choice is the one we made sometime in the past and that we make every day: our preoccupation with the egoic self and its vehicle, the body, and the environment and circumstances that surround our body and personality. Nature endows us with certain impulses and needs. We should not and, realistically, cannot ignore them without paying a price. But one of the consequences is that the world of the senses — our thoughts, emotions, memories, desires, fears, and reactions — eclipses the larger reality of life in which we live and breathe.

The complex matrix of our past choices exerts an unseen influence or shadow over our present actions. Most human choices for change are just rearranging the furniture of our karmic house. Some choices, including diet, exercise, and relationships, have the potential to contribute to our long-term spiritual awakening; others are simply neutral; while some are decidedly bad news. We must play the golf ball of life where it lies. We can't kick the ball unnoticed by God from out-of-bounds onto the fairway.

---

* Identifying himself with a shallow ego, man takes for granted that it is he who thinks, wills, feels, digests meals, and keeps himself alive, never admitting through reflection (only a little would suffice!) that in his ordinary life he is naught but a puppet of past actions (karma) and of nature or environment. Each man's intellectual reactions, feelings, moods, and habits are circumscribed by effects of past causes, whether of this or a prior life. Lofty above such influences, however, is his regal soul. —Paramhansa Yogananda, *Autobiography of a Yogi*

If we do, we get penalized. We can't, in other words, make choices that aren't offered to us by the matrix of our psychic software.

Even if we are currently pleased with our life circumstances, it remains true that "Chains though of gold still bind." Nor are any outward circumstances of health, wealth, status, or pleasure ever secure against the ravages of time, karma, and attack. We may shout our happiness to the skies but somewhere inside is a small voice of warning.

Happy or sad, we ourselves have created our own version of determinism. A woman saint in India described our freedom of choice using the analogy of riding a train: we can walk up and back through the train cars, but we can't change the direction or speed of the train.*

What I am hinting at is that "the only way out is in!" Transcendence of the ceaseless play of our own emotions, instincts, and restless thoughts brings to us inner peace. The tangible vibration of peace can infuse our daily activities with courage, calmness, confidence, and non-attachment. And the intuition to know what choices support that inner peace.

In a more philosophical vein, it may be helpful to remind ourselves that we, and all things in creation, are manifestation of the One. Eventually we must return to God because that's who and what we are. However, we still possess the choice to prefer the creation over oneness. We can choose to continue to wander for an eternity. But at some point, the "anguishing monotony"† of repeated rounds of birth, life, and death is going to find us wanting an "exit visa," and like the

* Ananda Moyi Ma: featured in Yogananda's autobiography.
† "Anguishing monotony" is a phrase from Chapter 30 ("The Law of Miracles") in *Autobiography of a Yogi*.

parable of the prodigal son we will begin to want to return to our "Father's home."*

Whether or not you subscribe to reincarnation, there is only one worthwhile choice to consider: Do we turn towards, or away from, God? Do we think of God, or not? Do we offer our thoughts and desires up for divine guidance, or not? Do we possess the faith and courage to follow the counsel given by our spiritual teacher or scripture, or not?

Once we turn towards God, we can even take advantage of our entanglement by humbly demanding God help us out of the matrix we have created. Why? Because we never asked to be created in the first place! Yogananda said God doesn't mind being addressed in this way and is inclined to give a helping hand when we recognize our need and our right to God's help.

There are many ways, of course, to hasten our soul's awakening. Spiritual teachings of East and West have always offered practical guidance. There's no denying the value of prayer, good deeds, righteous behavior and attitudes, kindness, and the Golden Rule. Good karma brings us closer to God than bad karma. Good karma is like having a clear night sky and powerful telescope to see the moon. But to fly to the moon takes something far greater. We must make the choice that the prodigal son makes in Jesus' story: to return home to his Father's house.

This final choice is the reverse of the original choice we made "way back when." We can rule the world but not rule our own mind. We can have everything, but not freedom from delusion, nor true love, nor lasting happiness. To achieve the purpose of our creation there must arise within

---

* The parable of the prodigal son can be found in Luke 15:11–32.

us the desire to know God and to enter the unfathomable, transforming, and unconditional love of the Creator.

Truth be told, for our final freedom we must want God as a drowning man wants air. Most of us are not quite there yet, but no matter. We can begin by wanting to know God because all our desires must be fulfilled. As our desire for God grows, we will magnetically draw the great, but ever so humble, power of the Universe to give us a hand along the Way.

PART THREE

Yoga and the East

Chapter 29

A New View of History

I S THERE AN OBJECTIVE BASIS FOR A NEW COVENANT OR dispensation? Could it be that sweeping changes in our understanding of spiritual truths are upon us? Is it possible that human understanding has been influenced by forces that we are not currently aware of? Is there truth to the belief held by ancient civilizations that prehistoric humanity once experienced a golden age of wisdom and harmony?*

There is a book I'd like to recommend to you. It challenges the commonly accepted view that humanity has ascended from ignorant cave men to the state of today's sophistication and accomplishment. That book is called *The Yugas*. The seminal inspiration for *The Yugas* is contained in the introduction to the book, *The Holy Science*, written by Yogananda's guru, Swami Sri Yukteswar.

In *The Yugas*, the authors explore Swami Sri Yukteswar's startling but succinct rewrite of human history. The book describes how each of humanity's great civilizations posits the concept that human consciousness goes through four stages

---

* It is a modern bias to equate intelligence with technology. Harmony with all life finds its highest expression in simplicity not complexity.

of increasing and decreasing intelligence and virtue. The four stages, or cycles, rise and fall in arcs of many thousands of years. In the Indian tradition these cycles are called *yugas* (or ages). The complete cycle, four epochs increasing and four decreasing, are aligned with the precession of the Equinox, a cycle of some 24,000 years.

According to his calculations based on Hindu astronomy, Swami Sri Yukteswar declared that on or about 1700 A.D. humanity entered a two-hundred-year transitional period into a new and ascending age of understanding called *Dwapara Yuga* (meaning the Second Age), the main body of which began about 1900 A.D.

Dwapara Yuga is still largely a materialistic age, but it is characterized by the growing perception that energy is the basis for matter and that everyone is worthy of self-respect and the right to pursue self-interest. My purpose for bringing up a subject that is admittedly new to many readers is that this understanding is the basis for the belief that humanity is moving slowly but inexorably toward greater awareness. That this is true in science and technology is unquestioned.* But fundamentalists in all religions feel just the opposite when it comes to human conduct, ethics, and morals.† How do we reconcile these two opposite trends in

---

* In this view of history, it is no coincidence that Einstein's great discoveries took place within the first ten or so years of Dwapara Yuga. In this age, Swami Sri Yukteswar explained (in the introduction to his book, *The Holy Science*) that humanity will demolish the dimension of space (think travel and communication) and will discover the finer electrical and atomic forces that underlie the appearance of matter. He, in effect, predicted Einstein's discovery, as well as an increasing average life expectancy, an increasing average height, and an astonishing increase in the quantity and pace of technological advancement.

† I don't want to provide a survey of discouraging views but I can say that many fundamental Christians speak of the end times, especially in relation to the breakdown of morals in society; Hindu fundamentalists speak of humanity living in a

human knowledge and behavior?

The dissolution of morals and ethics (as viewed by fundamentalists) is interpreted by Yogananda and his lineage as the necessary dissolution of old ways of thinking. The first age out of which we have come (called *Kali Yuga*) is characterized by fixity of form. Think of the rigidity of social status in the Middle Ages; consider too, the absolute and hereditary rule of kings; the fixed beliefs in religion and philosophy.

The Renaissance era in Western history marked the beginning of humanity's questioning of the fixed authority of *a priori* dogma. It was the beginning of artistic, natural, and world exploration. Then came the Protestant revolt and the beginnings of the age of science. We began to question, to explore, and to seek evidence for what was true rather than relying on preexisting central authority to tell us what is true.

But if it is true that the end times are upon us, or at least in front of us, there would be no point in doing anything new. In this case, we would have every reason, beginning with Jesus' own warnings against false prophets, to stay glued to the literal words of the Bible. The concept of the *yuga* cycles, then, is the objective basis for a new dispensation, which is to say, a new understanding of the teachings of Jesus Christ.

I cannot prove to a fundamentalist that Yogananda is not a false prophet or the Antichrist, that is up to the individual to decide. However, in the Bhagavad Gita, Krishna tells

four-hundred-thousand-year cycle of declining virtue; Moslem fundamentalists rail at Western morals; perhaps there are even Buddhist fundamentalists who feel humanity has lost its way compared to former times.

us that in every age God sends an *avatar* in response to the prayers of devotees to correct error and uphold truth.[*] As it seems obvious that humanity has entered a new era, it would seem the time is ripe for such a divine descent.

It takes an act of faith, in the face of Churchianity's dogmas to the contrary, to be open to the possibility that God, in the human form of Self-realized souls, comes to earth in every age to redirect human history and consciousness towards Truth. That humanity needs help is obvious. The intertwining of religions and cultures throughout the world and the dissolution of respect for traditional authority is wreaking havoc, chaos, and misery especially upon the soul-sensitive truth-seekers who yearn for deeper understanding and unity. If religion fails to act as a force for harmony, no other means exists. Politics, economics, education, science, and the arts all have a place in human civilization, but they cannot inspire and uplift humanity to a higher level of consciousness wherein respect, and harmony prevail. No other human endeavor apart from spirituality seeks to raise our consciousness. Other human pursuits may improve our material existence, provide some security, protection, stability, and continuity of culture, or give to us an appreciation of beauty, but none can inspire us to love God and to love one another as children of God.

Thus, it was at the very beginning of *Dwapara Yuga*, that Paramhansa Yogananda was born (in 1893) and was sent to the West.[†] He was not the only one. There were others, such

---

[*] Bhagavad Gita 4:6–7 "O Bharata, whenever virtue declines and vice predominates, I incarnate on earth. Taking visible form, I come to destroy evil and reestablish virtue."

[†] In the context of the description of history offered to us by the yugas, Jesus Christ appeared on earth in the waning centuries of the twelve-thousand-year

as Swami Vivekananda, who came with similar intent.

The view offered to us by the *yuga* cycles is that a new age of understanding and awareness has begun. Sweeping changes in human activity and human consciousness are just beginning. It is in this view that the appearance of a new world teacher and a new dispensation of spiritual understanding has its place in human history.

---

descending cycle which ends in the lowest age called *Kali Yuga*. At about 500 A.D., the ascending arc of *Kali Yuga* began. Not surprisingly, this roughly corresponds with the fall of Rome and the end of the classical age. The teachings of Jesus Christ therefore are seen, in the view of the *yugas*, as setting the stage for the beginning of the twelve-hundred-year span of ascending *Kali Yuga*.

Chapter 30

Esoterica of East and West

FOR THOSE WEANED ON THE RELIGIONS OF THE EAST, or for staunch believers of the New Testament, miracles are no big deal. For those wedded to science, miracles, despite the miracles of science itself, are poppycock. Yogananda has a chapter in his autobiography called "The Law of Miracles." Even though it is out of date in terms of more recent scientific discoveries, it offers some fascinating insights.

Yogananda often interpreted stories and teachings of the Bible from the perspective of individual spiritual awareness rather than as historical facts. The Star of Bethlehem, for example, he described as the inner star of light seen in the forehead behind closed eyes when in deep meditation. This star is sometimes called the Spiritual Eye* and is described as three concentric circles of gold, blue, and a central pinpoint of light (which when seen clearly becomes a five-pointed star). Meditators often see flashes or different shapes and colors of light in the forehead with the eyes closed, and sometimes with eyes opened.

---

* There are many other terms such as the Eye of Shiva; the Third Eye; Star of Wisdom.

Yogananda made the outrageous but curious claim that the three wise men were none other than his own line of guru-preceptors: Babaji, Lahiri Mahasaya, and Swami Sri Yukteswar (in their past lives and with different names). He explained that it was the inner spiritual eye that guided the three wise men from the East to Bethlehem.* At least one of the wise men is said to have been an astrologer. Yogananda's own guru, Swami Sri Yukteswar was a renowned astronomer and astrologer. To such wise men, the birth of Jesus would presumably have been revealed intuitively. They would have "seen" that a star — that is, an *avatar*, a world savior — was soon to be born. The location of the birth, too, would have been revealed. To travel far in order to honor such a person would be an appropriate act of devotion and recognition. This was the explanation that Yogananda gave.

Throughout the New and Old Testaments, we encounter people "bowing down and worshipping" the prophet. This custom still exists in India today, though to touch another's feet has expanded to include and be a more general sign of respect for parents and others. The burning of incense, washing the feet, baptism in the Ganges, waving of food before the altar, waving the hands to the forehead from over a candle flame, and many more customs suggest that Israel was more influenced by and connected to the East than to the West.†

---

* If you take the gospel's description of their journey it makes no sense on several counts: 1) If the star was seen in the East but they travelled East to West, did they have an eye in the back of their head? 2) What star rests over a building? A star is too far away to do anything but rest over everything. 3) No known astronomical phenomenon has been discovered to account for either the star or its unusual behavior.

† Apart from Rome, and consciously rejecting both Egyptian and Greek spirituality, there was nothing in the West that would have interested the Israelites.

Palestine was part of the Silk Routes and at the crossroads for trade between the East and the Roman empire
during the time of Jesus. The existence of an active and
profitable trade between India and the Roman Empire has
been confirmed by historians. We are told there were several
routes: the ocean route going south from the Mediterranean,
through the Red Sea, and sailing to the west coast of India; a
northern route above the Black Sea along the Asian steppes;
and the middle Eastern route through the Levant.* This latter
route would have been preferred because it is the most direct
route to India. It would have already been well established by
Alexander and the Greeks and many others in more recent
centuries. This route went through several ancient and so-
phisticated kingdoms.†

Jesus was not blond and blue-eyed. He was a Semite.
Many readers of the New Testament and of the life of Jesus
find it exceedingly odd that of his mere thirty-three years
of life, eighteen of them are unaccounted for (age twelve
through thirty). The first realistic but shocking account of
these missing eighteen years comes from a book by Nicolas
Notovitch (which I mentioned earlier) called *The Unknown
Life of Jesus Christ*. In his travels to the Far East, Notovitch
discovered scrolls that told of one called Saint Issa who traveled and studied in India and Tibet.‡ Around the proverbial

---

* Eastern Mediterranean including Syria to Palestine, approximately. The fact
that St. Thomas, the apostle, traveled to India via the southern route and ended
up all the way south and east in what is now Chennai is proof of the ready access
and knowledge of India that existed in Israel at the time of Jesus.

† Alexander's interest in yogis and gurus and their teachings is well known and
documented.

‡ The last verse (80) of Chapter 1 of Luke says simply that "the child grew, and
waxed strong in spirit, and was in the deserts till the day of his shewing unto
Israel." None of the other three Evangelists say anything at all.

campfire, Jesus would certainly have disclosed his journeys and experiences to his close disciples. Consider that Thomas the apostle traveled all the way to southern India in the years after Jesus' death. He was obviously aware of the existence of India and the spiritual potential and sophistication of her people.

Miracles such as healing the sick, raising the dead, casting out devils, and even resurrection after death have a rich history in the lore of India and the Far East.

One thing that strikes me as a curious connection between Roman culture and Jewish culture is the fascination with "the law." It is, in my view, ironic that Jesus, who crossed swords with the Pharisees over their obsession with the small details of Mosaic law, was to have his future followers create a mega-church based on Latin and comprised of a tangle of dogmas and ecclesiastical laws. The issue of the spirit (and meaning) vs the letter (literalness) of the law has continued to haunt Christianity to this day. Judas' betrayal of Jesus in favor of the power and status of the religious authorities has also been echoed in the history of Christianity.

Chapter 31

Prophecies

THE PROPHECIES OF THE RETURN OF JESUS TO EARTH are among some of the most confusing teachings of Christianity whether the prophecies are in the words of Jesus himself, his apostles, or his followers down through the ages. For starters, Jesus stated that "Verily I say to you, this generation shall not pass till all these things be fulfilled."* From this statement one would be forced to conclude that either these things did not happen, or they did happen in the first century and no one happened to notice.

Nature of Prophecy

I am no authority on prophecies but let me offer a perspective that I imagine. When a seer sees the future, the vision is drawn from the "ether" of timelessness, from the Akashic record, or from the superconscious state described previously. Superconsciousness is not circumscribed by past, present, or future, nor is its perspective a fixed or static one. It is one of possibilities and probabilities. Piercing its veil, the seer may return from the experience to describe events and

---

* Matt 24:34

scenes which bear little relationship to human experience or current culture. Superconsciousness is the region of what is possible. Its language is mythic and employs images and symbols. And the story is still being written. It is common to view prophecies as subject to change depending on intervening events and changes in human consciousness. Like our dreams, prophecies have a surreal quality to them.

Thus, the second coming prophecies which exist in Jesus' words, in Revelations, and in some of the epistles of the apostles are a combination of vision and speculation as to what is possible — they are not immutable predictions. As far as I can tell, only Jesus and St. John's descriptions can legitimately be assumed to have descended from a higher plane of consciousness. The epistles are, I believe, drawn from what Jesus revealed to the apostles.

No Man Knows When

Jesus himself admits he does not know the timing of these things: "But of that day and hour knoweth no man, no, not the angels of heaven, but my Father only."* Yet two verses previous he says that "this generation shall not pass away." Either Jesus was confused or his words had a meaning not susceptible to a literal interpretation. I suspect the latter.

Most of the "unpleasantness" described in the second coming prophecies can be viewed as events that haunt humanity constantly: wars, earthquakes, false teachers, conflicts among peoples, persecution of the faithful, and much more. It is therefore impossible to connect such happenings to any specific historical events.

* Matt 24:36

Destruction of the Temple

As it related to the "generation that shall not pass away," the temple of Jerusalem was destroyed by the Romans only thirty-eight years later. In fact, Jesus' initial prophecy was triggered when his disciples pointed out to him the majesty and beauty of the temple in Jerusalem. His initial words, then, seem to have been a response to the comments by his disciples in relationship to the temple of Jerusalem.* It is as if Jesus, hearing the words of the disciples who marveled at the sight of the temple edifice, turned to look at the temple but what *he* "saw" was not what the disciples saw with their human eyes, but a vision of the temple destroyed. To make the interpretation even more confusing, this exchange gets mixed up with Jesus' comments to the Pharisees, "Destroy *this* temple, and in three days I will raise it up!"† A non sequitur if there ever was one! This kind of mix of images and words is characteristic of prophecies.

Revelations and Yoga

St. John's revelations in the Apocalypse are another matter completely. So abstruse is his description, which involves monsters and beasts, one hardly knows what to do with it. It invites many interpretations and not all are eschatological. Paramhansa Yogananda took an entirely different tack, and one that is astonishingly coherent even if completely outside the lenses possessed by scholars and theologians; indeed, beyond anyone but the mystics of East and West.

Yogananda interpreted the first and last chapter of Revelations entirely from the perspective of the inner

---

* Matt 24:1, Mark 13:1, and Luke 21:5
† John 2:19

kingdom of consciousness as experienced in the astral body. He related the seven stars to the seven chakras taught in yoga. His analysis is surprisingly persuasive, but it only focuses on chapter one and the last chapter (twenty-two). Without his having said it, Yogananda's interpretation cannot suggest anything else for the rest of the Revelations other than a description of the soul's inner experience, not an eschatological one. I personally suggest we not take sides and consider that such a revelation might contain elements both in time (history) and in timelessness, which is to say being meaningful to individuals at any time in history. As stated in the Emerald Tablet of the Hermetic Texts, "as above, so below," we can view Revelations as a both-and reality: internal to the individual soul's experience and evolution and related to the history of humanity.

Indian Cycles of Time

As a side bar to the question of the end-times, one of the great teachings of *Sanatan Dharma* also includes the end of the universe (not just our world). The yuga cycles mentioned previously are just one of several concentric cycles of time taught in India since ancient times. Yogananda carried forward these teachings in his own writings when he described dissolution of the earth as being either partial or complete. The flood stories that abound throughout the cultures of earth would be described as partial dissolution. The largest time cycles are known as the Days and Nights of Brahma during which the cosmos itself is withdrawn and sent out again in epochs of many billions of years each.[*]

* The Bhagavad Gita speaks of such cycles in various chapters.

Once and Future Christ

Seven Churches

In my reading of Revelations and from my knowledge of the yoga teachings, the letters to the seven churches show clear parallels to the seven energy centers of the chakras.* Each epistle to one of the churches begins with praising the congregation and then administering a chastisement. In similar fashion, each chakra (energy center) has positive and negative aspects. In each letter to the churches there is some image or word that resonates with the traditional qualities or functions of one of the seven chakras as described in yoga treatises.

I conclude that these seven churches, whose cities are specifically identified, are very real and I assume the counsel given them was appropriate to their spiritual needs at that time. At the same time, I believe, and Yogananda's approach supports this, that St. John's vision simultaneously peers through a veil such that each of these churches represents one of the seven psycho-physiological energy centers of the astral body. It is as if his vision superimposed universal (human, astral) qualities onto the church and congregation. This is characteristic of superconscious inspiration. True scripture has the power to be timely while at the same time, timeless. Yogananda wrote that scripture applies on all levels: physical, mental, and spiritual.

Seven Spirits before the Throne

Other examples of the correspondence of St. John's vision and the teachings of yoga include his description of seeing Seven Spirits before the Throne of God. The first of these seven is the primordial Christ consciousness inherent

---

* An explanation of the astral energy centers is far beyond the scope of this book. There are innumerable explanations to be found online and in books.

in the creation. The six other Spirits are given responsibility for the three levels or realms of creation: physical, astral, and causal. Each realm has two Spirits assigned to it: one for the macrocosm of the realm and one for the microcosm of individual beings and objects which inhabit the realm. The causal sphere is the realm of ideation or thought. It operates by certain rules and within certain boundaries both as to the realm as a whole and to the causal beings who inhabit that world. The same is true of the astral realm and the physical world. All seven Spirits are manifestations of the innate and indwelling intelligence and intention of the Spirit (Father) beyond and untouched by the creation. The overarching "first" Christ consciousness thus divides itself into six subordinates to carry out the necessary functions of the three basic stages of creation.

Four Beasts and Twenty-four Elders

Another example can be found in the four beasts with eyes all around. Yogananda's guru, in his book *The Holy Science*, identifies these as the building blocks of creation in the form of time, space, and particle which emerge from the Holy Ghost (*AUM*) vibration or power. Thus the "voice" or vibration or outward flowing energy of God includes and forms the universal structure of energy, time, space, and object. These apply to both the astral and physical universes.*

The twenty-four elders before the throne are further identified as the twenty-four elements of creation and of the human body in all causal, astral, and physical manifestations:

---

* In Revelations, the faces of the four beasts are those of a lion, calf, man, and eagle. I would guess that the lion (the first) is the *AUM* vibration power; the calf symbolizes time; the man, the atom (individual); and the eagle, space.

five senses, five objects of the senses (objects of taste, touch, smell, hearing, and sight), five elements (earth, water, fire, air, space), five motions (feet, hands, excretion, procreation, and speech), plus four aspects of consciousness (ego, feeling, intelligence, and the mind linked to the senses).

The woman clothed by the sun is unquestionably the personification of *AUM*, the Divine Mother of creation and the goddess *Kundalini*. Satan is of course the dragon,* and of the two beasts one is the miracle-making Antichrist. I would speculate that the two beasts represent ego: one in a lower, perhaps animal form, and the other in the higher, intellectual form. The seven seals and seven angels and many other angels are the intelligence lieutenants of the angelic higher spheres who do the work of creation and carry out the will of God.†

Last Chapter of Revelations

The very last chapter of Revelations is "pure yoga."‡ From the throne (the cranial center of the seventh chakra on the top of the head) and from the Lamb (the soul) comes a pure river of water of life. The river is the astral spine, and the water is the life force (aka prana) that gives sustenance to the body (astral and physical). "On either side was there the tree of life with fruit trees" (the astral senses and objects). The central astral spine has two subsidiary channels on either side. The names of these channels in yoga teachings are *iḍa* and *pingala*. The movement

* I think the dragon could also be interpreted on the individual level as the negative form of *Kundalini*, coiled in rebellion and self-affirmation at the base of the human spine.

† See also the book, *The Holy Science*, by Swami Sri Yukteswar, Self-Realization Fellowship.

‡ Chapter 22, Revelations, 1–22. Yogananda *did* comment on this last chapter of Revelations.

of life force in the *iḍa* produces inhalation and in the *pingala*, exhalation.

"Blessed are these for they shall have access to the tree of life and may enter into the gates of the city" (the gates are the chakras which contain the powers of the soul). The morning star is Venus, the heart center.

It is interesting that Satan's defeat is only for a thousand years, after which he'll be let loose again. This could be a reference to the Night of Brahma, the dissolution of creation for a rest, prior to its reemergence. It suggests the continuation of the world* but should not be seen to suggest the individual soul never finds emancipation from delusion.†

Predictions by Yogananda

It is interesting to note that before his passing in 1952, Paramhansa Yogananda gave predictions of dire times ahead. Certain historical facts since 1952 could be seen as the fulfillment of parts of his predictions; others we might assume have not yet taken place; others still could be or already have been mitigated by those who have served the new dispensation he brought. All these, like the so-called prophecies of Nostradamus, as well as the Christian prophecies of the Second Coming of Christ, are difficult to interpret literally or to identify with specific, historical events.‡

---

* As spoken of earlier, duality (the play of opposites) is the necessary basis for the illusion of the creation to be perpetuated.

† Yogananda made the statement that a planet will be dissolved if its inhabitants become either entirely enlightened or wholly evil. He added that our Earth is mostly "rajasic" (meaning in between!).

‡ Yogananda spoke of the destiny of specific nations, wars, and widespread economic collapse. He also advised people to join with others to buy land outside the cities to grow their own food, and live a sustainable, prayerful, and serviceful life. These topics have been covered in books written by his many disciples, including Swami Kriyananda's, *The Road Ahead*.

Go Within

It is more useful to interpret Jesus' words and those of St. John from the perspective of your own, personal spiritual journey. Jesus' words especially can be viewed as counsel to uphold what Yogananda called the "first law of God:" loyalty. Stay loyal to your spiritual path, and tune into soul guidance while you avoid sin and evil. Be not distracted by the woes of this world and passing spiritual fads or false teachers. As Jesus put it, "Be wise as serpents and harmless as doves."*

The epistles written by the apostles contain a few references to Jesus' prophecies but do not add to them. St. John's Revelations can sound surreal, personal, historical, and abstract all at the same time, even like an LSD trip! When interpreted subjectively, Revelations takes on the character of a fantastic description of the soul's journey from heaven to earth, then to hell, and finally resurrection back into heaven. It can also be seen as the trajectory of human consciousness through many lives and through the cycles of time: beginning with the Garden of Eden, then to the Fall, onto the struggle between good and evil, and finally to the victory of the soul led by the Christ-consciousness.

Will the World Come to an End?

As to the question of the end times, or the end of the world, Yogananda's teachings indicate that no such end is in sight, based in part on his guru's recalibration of the yuga cycles. He did predict that the transitional period we have entered which involves the dissolution of an old-world order

* Matt 10:16

of consciousness would be a time of turmoil, chaos, and destruction. But the outcome would be a period of peace as
the new consciousness of inclusivity, cooperation, harmony,
and simple living takes hold. He did not say this period of
peace would last indefinitely since this age, *Dwapara Yuga*,
is still essentially a materialistic one and a certain amount of
chaos, insecurity, and ego-affirming self-interest are some of
its hallmarks.

Will Jesus Come Again?

Finally, Yogananda offered no comments on whether
or when Jesus would incarnate again, but the implication
from some of his words on general principles suggests that
Jesus has come already and will come again. As stated earlier, Yogananda called his mission in America "The Second
Coming of Christ." In retrospect this had to have been a very
bold assertion. I'm surprised he wasn't crucified one way
or another!* His explanation for the use of this term was
simply that whereas the Christ consciousness took human
birth in the form of Jesus, his return would take the form
of the awakening of the Christ consciousness in the hearts
of true devotees through the practice of meditation. This
follows the pattern of Jesus sending the Holy Spirit to the
apostles after his ascension into heaven to bring to their remembrance "all things."†

* Yogananda certainly had his troubles, however. He was dark-skinned, a Hindu,
and he spoke with great authority publicly about Jesus Christ and the teachings.
An account of Yogananda's life is available from author Phil Goldberg, *The Life
of Yogananda*.

† In teaching the technique he called the *AUM* technique, Yogananda equates
the inner communion with the primordial sound of *AUM* as the appearance of
the Holy Ghost vibration in human consciousness.

Awakening the Inner Christ

The role of the savior is, Yogananda taught, to awaken the Christ consciousness in the souls of those "who receive him." In Yogananda's use of the term "Second Coming of Christ," he wasn't necessarily saying he was fulfilling Jesus' prophecy of his return. It is worth adding, however, that he never denied it either. When asked he replied simply, "What difference would it make?"

It would be fair to say that his bringing the art and science of meditation, of inner communion, is the means through which the Christ consciousness is born in our hearts. Inner communion is the essence of what the outer communion of rituals like the Eucharist and various sacrifices are intended to evoke. It has been said that the role of the human guru is to awaken the inner guru of the soul. In this sense, then, the role of the Christ consciousness in human form (as the savior) is to awaken the Christ consciousness latent within us.

Recap and Summary

The underlying themes of our use of Yogananda's teachings are: 1) They represent an ancient yet timely and vibrant expression of eternal truths; 2) They turn us inward to experience spiritual consciousness directly through meditation; 3) Too much is made of the personhood of great souls like Jesus and it would be a betrayal of Yogananda's own teachings to merely set him (or Krishna, Buddha, etc.) up in place of Jesus; 4) The need and role of a savior, or "sat guru," is an integral part of the teachings of *Sanatan Dharma* and those of Christianity; 5) Admittedly, for his disciples, Yogananda is the sat guru but his lineage includes Jesus Christ; 6) The emphasis in this age, Dwapara Yuga, is upon self-effort. This is not a denial of the ultimate power of grace, but it emphasizes that grace comes in response to our efforts which must come of our own volition.

Chapter 32

The Three Bodies

IN *SANATAN DHARMA*, IT IS TAUGHT THAT ALL OBJECTS and aspects of creation have three concentric levels of reality: the physical, astral, and causal planes of existence. Every object contains each of these three levels.* Take for example, the human body. The obvious is the physical body; but there is also an energetic, or astral, body comprised of the life force, sometimes called "prana" or "chi," both subtle (vitality, for example) and gross (like brain waves or nerve pulses); and, finally, there is the thought, or causal, body. The causal body is the collection of ideas necessary for the initial intention to create, sustain, or dissolve any given object. In respect to the astral body there are some people who can see the outline of this astral body in the form of the aura. Saints are depicted with a nimbus, or halo, around their heads. This is a suggestion of their inner light. In the New Testament, Moses

* An especially perspicacious reader might wonder "Why three bodies" when all creation exists because of the principle of duality? We arrive at three bodies by separating the visible aspects of the Holy Ghost vibration from its energetic aspects. As an example, the visible aspect of vibration is the human body while the energetic vibration is the life and energy that inhabits it.

and Elias appeared to Jesus and the three of them were transfigured into their light, or astral, bodies and were seen in this form by the three disciples who were present.

This astral realm is the realm of the Holy Spirit, or *AUM* vibration as described earlier in this book. The causal realm is the sphere of the Christ consciousness. This Christ, or causal, intelligence is the "only begotten of the Father," meaning it is the reflected consciousness of the Spirit (who is beyond creation) and contains the intelligence, love, and intention necessary for the next stages or realms of creation. Of these three levels of reality, the energetic aspect is the link between consciousness and matter.*

An example of the distinction between the energy that animates matter and matter itself is seen in the distinction between a living person and a corpse. In the corpse the physical form (matter) exists but its life force has vanished.

That which unites and holds these in the form of a viable organism is individual ego-consciousness. Yogananda defined ego as the soul identified with the body and personality. He wrote that "the ego is an element of the astral body, which is retained after physical death. The physical body is merely the ego's projection into the material world." It is desire and willpower that brings these elements together into human form.

These three bodies interact seamlessly, and hence the ordinary person is unaware of their distinctive roles and their separate existences. Despite their working together they vibrate at very different frequencies. Just as my hand can't merge with a wall, I can't easily experience the three bodies

---

* Because only consciousness can perceive consciousness, science is left to deal with energy and matter.

independently.* Jesus did so, however, when he resurrected the three bodies over three days after his crucifixion.†

After what we call death, the other two bodies (causal and astral) live on and take with them the memory, including subconscious impressions, of the as-yet unfulfilled consequences of previous actions, unfulfilled desires, unresolved fears, and habitual tendencies.

Few humans ever wonder what animates the physical body. We are awake and we sleep. During wakefulness we are busy moving around, reacting emotionally, thinking, remembering, or imagining. At night we enter the world of dreams which, during our experience of it, is every bit as real to us as our waking state. In dreamless sleep, we remember nothing, but we nonetheless know that we have slept. During the day we are primarily aware of the physical body; at night, the astral body; in dreamless sleep we rest in the causal body.

The increasing volume and documentation of near-death experiences is just one testimony to the existence of consciousness independent of the body and brain. The testimony of Jesus Christ and rishis down through ages is another. But for the rest of us, meditation is the most practical and time-tested means to become more aware of these three bodies.‡ As our awareness becomes more inwardly

---

* In dreaming we are more completely in the energy, or astral, body. In dreamless sleep, we are more completely in the causal body; in activity, we are more completely in the physical body.

† Yogananda taught specifically that the symbolism behind the three days that it took Jesus to resurrect his body is a reference to the resurrection of the three bodies in sequence. This he taught was the meaning behind Jesus' admonition to Mary Magdelene not to touch his body as "I am not fully ascended." Mark 16:17

‡ One might assume that we are quite aware of our physical body, but yoga teachers, doctors, nurses, physical therapists, and fitness instructions can attest to how many people are quite unaware of their own physical body.

one-pointed with daily practice, the presence of the energy and thought bodies that inhabit the physical body become clearer to us.

PART FOUR

Looking Ahead

Chapter 33

A Thousand Words

THE DISCIPLES OF JESUS GOT FRUSTRATED WITH HIS endless parables.* In India, stories of Krishna and countless other rishis, kings, and warriors fill volumes of texts. The Old Testament is primarily cut from the same papyrus. We, like Jesus' disciples, prefer to have our medicine straight up but stories have a way of sticking around. And I understand that there is research that corroborates the power of narrative, not only to teach, but to be retained and passed on intact.

It may surprise us today, proud as we are of our literacy, our rationality, and our verbal acuity, that pictures really are worth a thousand words. In Yogananda's written lessons he liberally sprinkles his teachings with stories, and his now famous and popular autobiography is comprised of mostly captivating stories with deep philosophy sprinkled in and around them.

I find it interesting how technology has moved toward visual communication from its origins in the written word. I can remember when graphic interface technology revolutionized

* Matt 13:10

desktop computers. At first, I thought it was, well, "window dressing" — useless but pretty. But then I discovered its power in the arena of reporting and presentation, even of financial data, and I've never looked back. Prior to that discovery, my favorite Word processing software was Zywrite: a veritable flying gas can with no graphical memory-eating inhibitions and driven by lightning-fast key-stroke CTRL functions!

The day may come when we return to the days of pre-history in which the story and the power of telepathic transmission will return. In *The Yugas* book mentioned earlier it is averred that writing was invented primarily for trade and to bolster the declining power of memory. When saints meet each other, little is said but much is shared. Consider also the ratio of the number and length of commentaries on the Bible, the Bhagavad Gita, the Yoga Sutras, the Koran, and on Buddhist texts compared to the scriptures themselves. I rest my case.

I think in the centuries to come, the power of the narrative will increasingly become the medium of transmission of consciousness that it once was. The intellect tends to be dry and lacking in motivational power, which is to say heart quality. But a story, such as the Prodigal Son or the woman caught in adultery, touches our hearts. Like song, chant, music, and poetry, a story can reach more deeply into our psyche and soul and bypass our "Doubting Thomas" intellect. "Analysis is paralysis" it has been well said.

Chapter 34

Do I Need Religion?

BASED ON THE EARLIER DISCUSSION OF FREE WILL, IT would be natural to see "spiritual but not religious" as an obvious choice; indeed, many see it as a better choice than religion.

Religion receives and deserves a lot of brickbats. In India there is a teaching that for one to achieve God-realization one must help free at least six other people. The details aren't important, but the point is that the spiritual path cannot be walked alone or just for your own salvation. As another Indian proverb says, "It may be good fortune to be born into religion, but it is a misfortune to die in one." (To die, spiritually, that is.)

Jesus repeated the Old Testament commandments when he was asked to summarize his teachings: "Thou shalt love the Lord thy God with all your heart, mind, soul, and strength. This is the first and great commandment, and the second is like unto it: You shall love your neighbor as yourself."*

In India the term used is "*satsang*" and in Christianity

---

* Matt 22:34–40

the term is "fellowship." I subscribe to the idea that religion is "supportive spirituality." Yogananda said that the church is the "hive" and grace is the "honey." By grace he was referring to actual contact with God, especially through direct, inner perception in meditation. Both are needed. It is a rare person who is sufficiently spiritually advanced to live apart from others of like mind. Some in these days of anti-religion claim they can do so, but in fact, very few true hermits exist.*

Along the path there are those ahead of us, those with us, and those behind. "We are One," and those who truly love God will naturally feel that love and sympathy towards others. Sometimes, and especially in the yoga tradition, aloofness pretends to be spiritual. This is not non-attachment; it is indifference and is born of ego. True non-attachment ought to apply to ourselves: to our own, inner likes, dislikes, and delusions, not to the delusions of others. Yogananda as a young monk viewed organization as a "hornet's nest" of troubles but his guru chastised him for it. Yogananda then vowed to spend his life helping those who would receive his help.

We are helped by helping others just as we, in turn, have been helped by others. Our creative, dynamic, and committed service to a spiritual cause with others of like mind provides more upliftment than the small amount of time we can meditate deeply each day. Few can meditate for very long. Most must support themselves at the same time. But when meditation and service go hand in hand, each can energize and deepen the other.

Don't get me wrong: I'm not a big fan of religion. History has repeatedly shown religion's inclinations towards error,

* In the wonderful book, *Saints that Moved the World* (Rene Fulop-Miller), the story of St. Anthony of the desert is a worthy read about living alone and finding salvation.

pride, abuse, and exploitation. But what part of society hasn't? For that fact alone, we cannot evade the issue of our own need to contribute positively to society. So why exclude the one and only thing that matters to the soul and to all souls: spiritual awakening? As Yogananda's guru put it wryly: "Those too good for this world, are adorning some other. So long as you breathe the free air of earth, you are under obligation to render grateful service."

In my life I have seen that those who reject spiritual fellowship and selfless service in the name of a higher spiritual goal do not find it.

As our body might be seen as either a "necessary evil," or, as "a channel to God," the same can be said of religion. If you are inclined to reject religion, I recommend that you look more closely within yourself for the reasons and be wary of claiming you are on a higher path.

Chapter 35

The Once and Future Christianity

TRUTH IS A HOLOGRAM: IN WHATEVER FORM YOU encounter it, it can be a portal to other aspects if you look carefully. There are truths hidden in the Bible that are there to be found when we "have eyes to see and ears to hear" as Jesus put it so often. The future of Christianity is hidden in its past. So here are some of the trends in evolving awareness that I think will help Christianity to accept other faiths and to profess a more universal understanding of the life and teaching of Jesus Christ.

Personal Relationship with God. A pivotal idea that will move Christianity forward is a growing understanding that our personal relationship with God is the essence of faith. From this understanding comes a lessening emphasis on sacraments and rituals; or, put conversely, that the purpose of sacraments and dogma is to encourage us to deepen our faith and direct perception of God's presence in our lives.

Wordless prayer, silent communion and meditation will find increasing acceptance.

The Sons of God. Increasingly, scholars and theologians, examining the testimony of the saints and the words of Jesus, will discover that the concept of the "only begotten son of God" is not limited to the human form and life of Jesus Christ but exists latently in all people and has appeared in fully Self-realized humans down through human history.

Original Sin. An understanding may grow that "original sin" isn't limited to a regrettable decision by two human beings, the so-called first parents, but is the choice of origin made by each of our souls at the time of our creation by God. Furthermore, this choice will be seen as one that most souls make at the time of puberty and every day of our lives thereafter.

What is Sin? Seeing sin as ignorance and its consequences as karma to be worked out will provide an incentive as well as hope.

Ego Transcendence. A new perspective on the significance of Jesus accepting God's will in undergoing crucifixion might be to accept our trials and tribulations as opportunities to work towards ego transcendence. It is the ego and personality that fears or spurns "crucifixion." The soul welcomes release from the prison of ego and body-consciousness. (I think of St. Francis who called his body "Brother Donkey.") Jesus' act of redemption is the act that each soul is invited to imitate. There's no "free ride" in that Jesus' crucifixion does something for us that we do not have to do as well. He will give us the grace, which is to say the power, to do that which, on our own, we cannot do. The ego and body are all we know and have. It makes no sense for the ego-body to "kill" itself. This goes against our deepest instinct. It is by grace that we "see the light of the soul" and work towards that light by combining self-effort and grace. It's not that a single historical act (of crucifixion) on its own constitutes and transmits that power. However, that historical act illustrates the heroic courage being asked of the soul on the journey to salvation.

Universal Christ-Consciousness. An understanding that Christ is not just the person of Jesus, but a universal and ever-present consciousness poised to pour out to us the transforming power of divine love to those who will "receive."

Importance of Reincarnation. An eternity of damnation, as a teaching and reality, is already growing in disfavor among refined and thoughtful people. Reincarnation is the solution. Hell is something we make of life whether in a human body or in the astral afterlife by our own actions and our rejection of God and goodness in others. Furthermore, the afterlife states, whether heavenly or hellish, will be viewed as temporary waystations not permanent states. This will bring great hope and encouragement to many. I hope that scholars will begin to find references and connections in the historical records of the teaching of reincarnation during the Christian era. Research on the validity of reincarnation grows every year.

Divine Union. Union with God, and not just eternal confinement in a familiar ego, will become better understood by more people. Liberation from ego and union with God will be seen as the promise of immortality and the goal of emancipation from rebirth. Union will not be seen as a threat, but a promise of eternal life and bliss.

Other Christ-like Saviors. Those souls born into and drawn to Jesus Christ as their guru will be able to love God and find liberation through Jesus even as they can accept that other souls, entire families of souls, find that freedom through the guru given to them (such as Krishna, Buddha, etc.) The tension or uneasiness born of having to embrace a religion that excludes others will steadily dissipate.

God is the Guru. More sincere seekers will be open to the idea that there can be more than one savior, and thus will hopefully be less resistant to the idea of discipleship as they come to the deeper realization that, as Yogananda put it, "God is the guru." The guru is a soul like you and me, but the guru has achieved Self-realization in a former lifetime. The guru's crowning success becomes an achievement that we, too, can aspire towards. History shows us that there have been many such saviors. The guru's life and teachings become more personal and accessible. The guru's attunement with God eases the inclination to make God in our image, which is to say, in an anthropomorphic form.

God's Handiwork of Creation is Good. Seeing that a human can be God-realized will also begin to erode the belief that the body and the creation are inherently evil. God intended from the beginning that souls could live and enjoy for a time God's creation in human form. We see that affirmed in the story of the garden of Eden. As God is beyond the creation, so too the soul lives on; but as God *is* the creation, so too we can achieve Self-realization without rejecting God's handiwork.

God's Mercy and Love

Consider this quote from the Old Testament, from the Book of Ezekiel.[*]

> But if the wicked will turn from all his sins that he hath committed, and keep all my statutes, and do that which is lawful and right, he shall surely live, he shall not die. All his transgressions that he hath committed, they shall not be mentioned unto him: in his righteousness that he hath done he shall live.

In the first few decades of the twentieth century there lived in Poland a humble nun called Sister Faustina.[†] She had many conversations with Christ and visions of the heavenly realms. After her death in 1938, she effectively, though not literally, founded a new religious order whose purpose, at the command of Jesus, was to emphasize God's mercy rather than divine justice (i.e., punishment). In her diary she recorded Jesus' words to her: "In the Old Covenant I sent prophets wielding thunderbolts to My people. Today I am sending you with My mercy to the people of the whole world. I do not want to punish aching mankind, but I desire to heal

---

[*] Ezekiel 18:21

[†] It was the Polish pope, John Paul II who was instrumental in her recognition. She was canonized as a saint in the year 2000.

it, pressing it to My Merciful Heart" (Diary, 1588). Perhaps this is a signal to the Catholic Church of a new dispensation of forgiveness and mercy rather than eternal hellfire?

Chapter 36

Rise of Individualism

AS DESCRIBED IN THE GROUNDBREAKING BOOK mentioned earlier (*The Yugas*), the age in which we now live is an age of the rise of individualism. As Swami Sri Yukteswar put it in *The Holy Science*, humankind is gaining in self-respect. That's a somewhat quaint term, but for most of us today personal liberty, individual rights, and respect for the individual are unassailable dogmas.

The famous post-war Nuremburg Trials of Nazis accused of war crimes established the concept that obedience to authority was not justification for crimes against humanity. This signaled a shift in human consciousness from the older era of *Kali Yuga* to the next and second era of *Dwapara Yuga* ("Dwa" means second). The age of empires and kings was rapidly dissolving in favor of an age of individual human rights.

It is no coincidence (to some of us, at least) that in the arena of spirituality, "spiritual but not religious" would appear as a growing trend; or, that the practice of yoga and meditation would effectively symbolize the individual's personal search for God and for meaning and self-worth; and that the concept of "Self-realization" would increasingly appear in print and common usage. All of this portends an emphasis upon the individual's search for God and the need for self-effort.

This contrasts with the emphasis, in the former "medieval" age, that God is a King, and we are serfs who, because of original sin, live in bondage. We can only be freed by the grace of God through his Son. Not surprisingly, this was how society was organized during such times.

There are only two aspects to spiritual awakening, and both are necessary: self-effort and divine grace. At different points on the journey, one is emphasized more than the other. I have already written at length in this book on both, but in general, self-effort is becoming the primary emphasis in this age.

Naturally, the outcome of a shift in emphasis from being a lowly, nameless serf fulfilling the duties of one's station in life to an expectation of having choices and personal interests has the potential to produce chaos and selfishness to an unprecedented degree.

The breakdown in personal morals, ethics, and behavior is epidemic. Traditional religionists therefore see the world coming to an end because of the predictable divine retribution that will follow. What fundamentalists don't notice however, is the growing interest in personal authenticity. Because fundamentalists take their life-cues from the rules given to them, they find it difficult to imagine that personal authenticity could be anything but a sham created by the great Deceiver.

However, a sincere effort to be authentic cannot but turn inward. Intuition will be the fulcrum point at which East and

West will meet. Inspiration, which is intuition, comes to us from the higher realm which is the source of all life. In that realm we are united. Yogananda's core message and the message of freedom everywhere is that we are all part of a greater reality. The message behind ecological awareness is similar, at least on a natural level. At the same time, we are each a unique expression of that greater reality. Yes, you guessed it: "Both-And."

The Yuga cycle theory as revitalized and recalibrated by Swami Sri Yukteswar sheds a different light upon this apparent mass breakdown of human conscience. Consider as an example that in the past you would follow the occupation of your father or even grandfather. But these days fewer and fewer people build their identity around the work they do, whether it be engineer, doctor, or parent. Tribal bonds of family, religion, language, culture, or nationality are in the process of rapid disintegration. The nuclear family unit is being replaced by the "blended family" of stepparents, stepsiblings, and global family connections.

All of this represents a breakdown of traditional bonds of security and identification. This Age of the Individual (as I like to call it) makes it seem, at first, easy to turn one's back on God in favor of your own convenience or opinion. But the truth, in the end, will always surface.

If Jesus Christ or a Christ-like savior were to appear today, how much impact would he or she have? Resistance or indifference to discipleship is, I believe, a growing phenomenon. How many living saints do we hear about today? As a young Catholic boy, I used to exclaim to God, my soul, and myself, "Where have all the saints gone? Where is Jesus Christ when we need him?"

When I review what I have written regarding how Christianity might expand its self-identity, it seems both natural and right, but I still puzzle over the *how*. On the one hand a new covenant would seem to only be possible with a new *avatar* (savior). If you imagine that I am about to propose that Paramhansa Yogananda qualifies for the role, you are correct, but that is only a personal view and not necessary for what I wish to share in this book.

Besides, it seems very unlikely that the hierarchy of any major Christian denomination would look to Yogananda as a messenger from Jesus Christ. Given the growing indifference to beliefs and to discipleship among people in general, it also seems untimely. Add to this that Christianity, though large in numbers of adherents, is woefully fractured.[*]

Yogananda himself, though quite a promoter in his "barnstorming" days of the 1920s and 1930s, was nonetheless low-key in many other respects. His now-famous autobiography is a collection of stories and spiritual teachings that seem to have omitted the author from any personal consideration. The bare facts of his life story are present in his book like the beams of a building, but it takes a sensitive reader to intuit the spiritual magnetism and power of the author. Yogananda's own lineage in the ninetheenth and twentieth centuries were themselves very low key in public terms.[†]

At this time in history, the evolution of human consciousness towards greater awareness requires that individual self-effort needs to be emphasized. Too strong a focus on the personality of a saint or *avatar* will not serve the spiritual

---

[*] Estimates of the number of Christian denominations worldwide vary considerably from 9,000 to over 40,000. Nothing and no one can unite these fractious sects anytime soon.

[†] Swami Sri Yukteswar, Lahiri Mahasaya, and Mahavatar Babaji.

awakening of most people. Yoga and meditation as spiritual practices require self-discipline and self-effort and thus are ideal symbols of this evolution. Discipleship will continue to attract, well, "disciples," but mass consciousness, it seems to me, is not going to head in this direction for a very long time.

For these reasons, I think the transformation of Christianity will be from the ground up. Such a transformation is appropriate to this age of democracy. Organizations, however, like individual organisms, also have a survival instinct. As mainline Christian churches see a continuing decline in membership, their leaders will eventually discover some of the key points I have identified as existing, albeit previously unnoticed, in their own teachings from the beginning. They will then proclaim these points, or, more likely, simply admit them into their narrative. Like ordaining women priests, it will suddenly seem to be the obvious thing to do. Hence the relative unlikelihood that a great savior or saint will appear to endorse a more expanded and universal understanding of the life and teachings of Jesus Christ. The internet aptly symbolizes the importance of the individual and individual access to information, including a book like this one.

Yogananda will, nonetheless, have played an important role and will, I think, be recognized as having done so by many people in the decades and centuries to come. It is wholly democratic and in tune with our age to see Christ universal in everyone. Why confine Christ to one person who lived only thirty-three years over two thousand years ago in a somewhat backwater province of the mighty empire of Rome! Ironically, and accepting that there will be hairsplitting differences of expression, I believe it will be found true that this has been taught by true Christians since A.D. 33.

Chapter 37

Our Return Journey

W E, IN OUR EGOS, HAVE REJECTED AND CRUCIFIED God's son within us by our ignorance, indifference, and endless desires for material and egoistic satisfactions. Our nature impels us to seek the happiness we once had in the Father but the convenience and easy accessibility of the senses tempts us with opportunities to forget our true parentage. We have eaten the apple from the tree of knowledge of good and evil by choosing the creation and its ceaseless dualities for our reality. We seek happiness from the creation rather than from its Maker. We are that prodigal child who takes our inheritance of intelligence, will, and choice into foreign lands of sense and matter indulgence. We eventually squander our life force (our inheritance) in wrong living. When we at last find ourselves in the gutter of despair and disillusionment, we remember the long-lost harmonious household of God-consciousness. Then, we resolve to undertake the arduous journey back to our home in God.

But let's look at that "gutter" for a moment. Many devotees and truth-seekers would object saying, "I'm not in the gutter. I've been very successful, intelligent, and energetic.

My interest is in finding truth!" But I ask you, "If your life is all that good why are you interested in something more?" Here's one of the many ironies or paradoxes of the spiritual path: life must be good enough for us to have the opportunity to think more deeply, to find the time and energy for spiritual practices but not so good that we are smug and unaware of just how fragile a thing is life and material success.

If life destroys our health, security, reputation, home, and loved ones, what great sacrifice is it for us to finally turn to God? Admittedly, this is the most common reason for people to pray. "There are no atheists in foxholes" it was said during the world wars of the twentieth century. I'm not referring to the times when we cry out in pain and resort to prayer for relief. With compassion, I recognize this is a common occurrence, but under those circumstances people want relief from suffering; we want the health or wealth that we had before; we are not seeking the love of God for its own sake.*

On the other hand, if I am at the top of the game of life and I realize that I am not happy, then I have truly learned something important. By contrast, if I am wholly defeated by life, I am not likely to turn fully to God. Why? Because my very defeat means I failed to attain the fulfillment I was seeking. That failure constitutes an unfulfilled desire. My karma is thus not finished.†

By contrast, consider the devotee, like Job in the Old Testament, whose life is abundant with material blessings.

---

* In the Bhagavad Gita VII:3, Krishna states that "Out of a thousand, (only) one seeks Me."

† It is possible that with a strong affirmation of will fired with soul wisdom and divine grace, I can dissolve the attachment to my failure and be free of the karmic consequences. Unfortunately, however, the usual reaction is to wallow in our defeats and identify ourselves with our failures.

Job has his faith tested when his health, wealth, and family are taken from him. Yet against the taunts of his neighbors who insist his losses were the result of his unfaithfulness to God, he holds steadfast in his faith and his insistence that he has lived a righteous life. Life's challenges can be tests of faith for one who already has some commitment to seeking God, even if that commitment arose in a past life. The dormant seed of that wisdom is watered by the rain of current difficult circumstances. As a result, both suffering and success are part and parcel of the soul's long journey home. This is one of life's many ironies.

Chapter 38

Future of Religion

MEDITATION HAS COME TO HELP US TRANSCEND sectarianism and discover for ourselves how each one of us can have a direct perception of the divine and a personal relationship with God. This does not mean that meditation, including Yogananda's own teachings and the core technique that he brought from India (called *Kriya Yoga*), will replace existing faiths such as Christianity. Instead, Yogananda predicted that in the centuries to come religionists of all faiths will come to view their religion and spiritual life as directed towards direct perception rather than hinging exclusively on dogma, beliefs, humanitarian work, and rituals. Meditation is the obvious tool for that direct perception. Its rapid spread around the world is proof enough, I feel, for the truth of his statement.

The way Yogananda expressed his prediction was in words such as "Self-realization will become the religion of the future." But he could not have meant this in a merely organizational sense because his own attitude and teachings simply preclude such a view. Neither does commonsense endorse it. The very meaning of the term "Self-realization" precludes an organizational enclosure.

There will be, of course, as there already are, those souls who will come to see Yogananda and the lineage that sent him as their own faith. "This is not a new religion," Yogananda said, "It is a new dispensation." Yogananda insisted that his work was not a new sect. While technically this cannot be true since he founded an organization and other organizations have proliferated, but what he surely meant was that it would *not* be *sectarian* in attitude and consciousness. But the future will take care of itself, however obvious this trend seems to me and others.

I am not alone in the depth of my gratitude for Paramhansa Yogananda. He came to America at great personal sacrifice and made tremendous efforts to reach the hearts and minds of thousands of Americans. However, without the lifelong, unstinting efforts of Swami Kriyananda, my teacher and a disciple personally trained by Yogananda, I could never have imbibed even the small glass of wisdom I have been privileged to sip if I had only had available to me the written lessons or books by Yogananda.

"The time for knowing God has come" thundered Yogananda more than once from the lecture platform. And I would add, the time for knowing God as *one* in all people and all faiths has also come. How can the blessings of a great world teacher like Jesus Christ be limited to a privileged few whose salvation is assured, while billions of others are damned for eternity? So, indeed, the time *has* come for a new understanding, a new dispensation for the "healing of the nations."[*]

* Revelation 22:2

Afterword

Who Is Paramhansa Yogananda?

I 'D LIKE TO EXPRESS A FEW THOUGHTS ON PARAMHANSA Yogananda. I consider myself a disciple of Yogananda and of the lineage of yogis who sent him to the West. I pretend, therefore, to have no scholarly objectivity. What I have noticed in my wide-ranging studies of so-called Eastern teachings (whether Hindu, Buddhist, or yogic) is that Yogananda is not frequently mentioned. Phil Goldberg's book, *The Life of Yogananda*, gives an objective acknowledgement of Yogananda's importance in the dissemination of yoga teachings. Naturally I would be thrilled if Yogananda received the public acclaim that I feel he deserves, but this has not been the case in the seventy years since his passing in 1952.

There have been celebrities such as Steve Jobs and George Harrison who had high praise for Yogananda and/ or his autobiography. Notwithstanding their endorsement, I liken Yogananda's relative obscurity to that of the sages of old whose names are not associated with the biographies of any historical person. The great scriptures of India, which in number, comprise millions of pages, are priceless.

We don't really know who Byasa or Patanjali were, for example.* Yogis with such names came and went and came again throughout India's history. Furthermore, as described earlier in this book, ours is an egalitarian age wherein all are equal. And although we could certainly use some heroes, we would probably bury them in imagined scandals. Yogananda decried the "yellow journalism" of his day which could destroy a person's reputation in a heartbeat for the sake of a headline and sale of newspapers.

We can see that yoga and meditation, and concepts like karma and reincarnation, are circling the globe at a furious pace, while belief in eternal damnation or salvation is on the wane. Yogananda is the one who brought Kriya Yoga to the West, and it is spreading like wildfire. I've not made any detailed references to the practices of meditation, though I have taught meditation including Kriya Yoga for decades. Ironically, Yogananda taught that it is meditation that reconciles East and West (rather than dogma). Yet this book is not intended to give instruction in how to meditate.

Another aspect of Yogananda's life work was a clarion call for the spread of intentional communities. Swami Kriyananda, trained by Yogananda, was the founder of the first of what became a network of intentional communities worldwide inspired by Yogananda's prediction that they, too, would spread like wildfire. Based on simple living and what he called "high thinking," Yogananda evidently foresaw the need for humanity to move toward a more sustainable and less materialistic way of life. We at Ananda like to think of

* Byasa transcribed the massive epic, *Mahabharata*, of which but one chapter comprises the beloved Hindu "bible," the Bhagavad Gita. He is also considered to be the author of many other famous works. Patanjali is said to be the author of now famous but succinct treatise on yoga called the Yoga Sutras.

Yogananda as the "patron saint of communities" for modern times. But these subjects (meditation and communities) are not the purpose of this book, so I have chosen to omit them.

Yogananda taught that meditation is a practice of inner communion and, as such, it is the vehicle for the fulfillment of Jesus' promise to return. But he, and later, Swami Kriyananda, spent considerable energy giving to the West the much-needed background and explanation before millions would be ready to seek this inner realization. Following their example, I have chosen to employ what Swami Kriyananda called "sweet reason" to share Yogananda's message of the underlying similarity between the teachings of Jesus (in the New Testament) and those of Krishna (in the Bhagavad Gita). This has been the sole purpose of my book.

Acknowledgements

This book could not exist without the grace of Paramhansa Yogananda and the wisdom of Swami Kriyananda. For direct assistance, editorial, and encouragement I want to thank Nayaswami Padma, my wife, and two editors with major input and suggestions: Dr. Rebecca Davis of Lynnwood, WA and Nancy Callan, Bothell, WA. Plus Nayaswami Dharmadevi and the Crystal Clarity staff for their support and focused efforts to bring this to fruition!

Nayaswami Hriman

Bibliography

Goldberg, Philip. 2020. *The Life of Yogananda*. New York: Hay House, Inc.

Kriyananda, Swami. 2004. *Intuition for Starters*. Commerce: Crystal Clarity Publishers.

—. 2011. *Paramhansa Yogananda: A Biography*. Commerce: Crystal Clarity Publishers.

—. 2009. *Religion in the New Age*. Commerce: Crystal Clarity Publishers.

—. 2009. *The New Path*. Commerce: Crystal Clarity Publishers.

—. 1973. *The Road Ahead*. Commerce: Crystal Clarity Publishers.

Kriyananda, Swami, and Paramhansa Yogananda. 2008. *The Rubaiyat of Omar Khayyam Explained*. Commerce: Crystal Clarity Publishers.

Lewis, C.S. 1952. *Mere Christianity*. London: Geoffrey Bles.

Selbie, Joseph, and David Steinmetz. 2010. *The Yugas*. Commerce: Crystal Clarity Publishers.

Yogananda, Paramhansa. 1926. *Advanced Course on Practical Metaphysics*.

—. 1946. *Autobiography of a Yogi*. Commerce: Crystal Clarity Publishers.

—. 2004. *Conversations with Yogananda*. Commerce: Crystal Clarity Publishers.

—. 1934. Original Praecepta Lessons.

—. 1990. *The Essence of Self-Realization*. Commerce: Crystal Clarity Publishers.

—. 2006. *The Essence of the Bhagavad Gita*. Commerce: Crystal Clarity Publishers.

—. 2008. *Whispers from Eternity*. Commerce: Crystal Clarity Publishers.

Yukteswar, Swami Sri. 1990. *The Holy Science*. Los Angeles: Self-Realization Fellowship.

1994. *Forrest Gump*. Directed by Robert Zemeckis.

About the Author

Nayaswami Hriman McGilloway was raised in a devout Catholic family and environment. With sixteen years of Catholic education, including two years at a preparatory high school seminary for the priesthood, Hriman has retained his love and respect for the core values and teachings of traditional Christianity. It was during his college years at the University of Santa Clara (a Jesuit college in the Bay Area of California), that the teachings of India and the practice of meditation came into his life. In his mid-twenties, Hriman traveled overland from Europe to India in search of India's timeless wisdom. Upon his return after over a year of travel, Hriman was introduced to Paramhansa Yogananda's now classic life story, *Autobiography of a Yogi*. Thereafter he met Swami Kriyananda, founder of the Ananda Community in northern California and a disciple of Yogananda, personally trained by him. For the last forty-five years, Hriman has practiced the Kriya Yoga taught by Yogananda and has shared with hundreds of students the precepts and practices of meditation. Since 1993 he and his wife, Padma, have served as the spiritual directors of Ananda Sangha in Washington State.

Further Explorations

CRYSTAL CLARITY PUBLISHERS

If you enjoyed this title, Crystal Clarity Publishers invites you to deepen your spiritual life through many additional resources based on the teachings of Paramhansa Yogananda. We offer books, e-books, audiobooks, yoga and meditation videos, and a wide variety of inspirational and relaxation music composed by Swami Kriyananda.

See a listing of books below, visit our secure website for a complete online catalog, or place an order for our products.

crystalclarity.com

800.424.1055 | **clarity@crystalclarity.com**

1123 Goodrich Blvd. | Commerce, CA 90022

ANANDA WORLDWIDE

Crystal Clarity Publishers is the publishing house of Ananda, a worldwide spiritual movement founded by Swami Kriyananda, a direct disciple of Paramhansa Yogananda. Ananda offers resources and support for your spiritual journey through meditation instruction, webinars, online virtual community, email, and chat.

Ananda has more than 150 centers and meditation groups in over 45 countries, offering group guided meditations, classes and teacher training in meditation and yoga, and many other resources.

In addition, Ananda has developed eight residential communities in the US, Europe, and India. Spiritual communities are places where people live together in a spirit of cooperation and friendship, dedicated to a common goal. Spirituality is practiced in all areas of daily life: at school, at work, or in the home. Many Ananda communities offer internships during which one can stay and experience spiritual community firsthand.

For more information about Ananda communities or meditation groups near you, please visit **ananda.org** or call 530.478.7560.

The Original Works of Paramhansa Yogananda

THE ORIGINAL 1946 UNEDITED
EDITION OF YOGANANDA'S
SPIRITUAL MASTERPIECE

AUTOBIOGRAPHY OF A YOGI
Paramhansa Yogananda

Autobiography of a Yogi is one of the world's most acclaimed spiritual classics, with millions of copies sold. Named one of the Best 100 Spiritual Books of the twentieth century, this book helped launch and continues to inspire a spiritual awakening throughout the Western world.

Yogananda was the first yoga master of India whose mission brought him to settle and teach in the West. His firsthand account of his life experiences in India includes childhood revelations, stories of his visits to saints and masters, and long-secret teachings of yoga and Self-realization that he first made available to the Western reader.

This reprint of the original 1946 edition is free from textual changes made after Yogananda's passing in 1952. This updated edition includes bonus materials: the last chapter that Yogananda wrote in 1951, also without posthumous changes, the eulogy Yogananda wrote for Gandhi, and a new foreword and afterword by Swami Kriyananda, one of Yogananda's close, direct disciples.

Also available in Spanish and Hindi from Crystal Clarity Publishers.

SCIENTIFIC HEALING AFFIRMATIONS
Paramhansa Yogananda

Yogananda's 1924 classic, reprinted here, is a pioneering work in the fields of self-healing and self-transformation. He explains that words are crystallized thoughts and have life-changing power when spoken with conviction, concentration, willpower, and feeling. Yogananda offers far more than mere suggestions for achieving positive attitudes. He shows how to impregnate words with spiritual force to shift habitual thought patterns of the mind and create a new personal reality.

Added to this text are over fifty of Yogananda's well-loved "Short Affirmations," taken from issues of *East-West* and *Inner Culture* magazines from 1932 to 1942. This little book will be a treasured companion on the road to realizing your highest, divine potential.

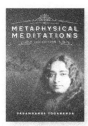

METAPHYSICAL MEDITATIONS
Paramhansa Yogananda

Metaphysical Meditations is a classic collection of meditation techniques, visualizations, affirmations, and prayers from the great yoga master, Paramhansa Yogananda. The meditations given are of three types: those spoken to the individual consciousness, prayers or demands addressed to God, and affirmations that bring us closer to the Divine.

Select a passage that meets your specific need and speak each word slowly and purposefully until you become absorbed in its inner meaning. At the bedside, by the meditation seat, or while traveling — one can choose no better companion than *Metaphysical Meditations*.

HOW TO BE HAPPY ALL THE TIME
The Wisdom of Yogananda, Volume 1
Paramhansa Yogananda

Yogananda explains everything needed to lead a happier, more fulfilling life. Topics include: looking for happiness in the right places; choosing to be happy; tools, techniques, and methods for achieving happiness; sharing happiness with others; and balancing success with happiness.

In the "Wisdom of Yogananda" series, Paramhansa Yogananda's timeless wisdom is offered here in an approachable, easy-to-read format. The writings of the Master are presented with minimal editing to capture his expansive and compassionate wisdom, his sense of fun, and his practical spiritual guidance.

THE NEW PATH
My Life with Paramhansa Yogananda
Swami Kriyananda

Winner of the 2010 Eric Hoffer Award for Best Self-Help/Spiritual Book

Winner of the 2010 USA Book News Award for Best Spiritual Book

The New Path is a moving revelation of one man's search for lasting happiness. After rejecting the false promises offered by modern society, J. Donald Walters found himself (much to his surprise) at the feet of Paramhansa Yogananda, asking to become his disciple. How he got there, trained with the Master, and became Swami Kriyananda makes fascinating reading.

The rest of the book is the fullest account by far of what it was like to live with and be a disciple of that great man of God.

Anyone hungering to learn more about Yogananda will delight in the hundreds of stories of life with a great avatar and the profound lessons they offer. This book is an ideal complement to *Autobiography of a Yogi*.

CONVERSATIONS WITH YOGANANDA
Stories, Sayings, and Wisdom of Paramhansa Yogananda
Recorded with reflections, by his disciple, Swami Kriyananda

For those who enjoyed Paramhansa Yogananda's autobiography and long for more, this collection of conversations offers rare intimate glimpses of life with the Master as never before shared.

This is an unparalleled account of Yogananda and his teachings written by one of his foremost disciples. Swami Kriyananda was often present when Yogananda spoke privately with other close disciples, received visitors and answered their questions, and dictated and discussed his writings. He recorded the Master's words, preserving a treasure trove of wisdom that would otherwise have been lost.

These Conversations include not only Yogananda's words as he spoke them, but the added insight of a disciple who spent over fifty years attuning his consciousness to that of his guru.

The collection features nearly five hundred stories, sayings, and insights from the twentieth century's most famous master of yoga, as well as twenty-five photos — nearly all previously unreleased.

THE YUGASA

Keys to Understanding Our Hidden Past, Emerging Energy Age, and Enlightened Future

Jsoeph Selbie and David Steinmetz

Many people lament the pace, and results, of the kaleidoscopic changes taking place in the world. Though our times show rapid changes, the cycle of the yugas shows us, reassuringly, that these changes are not random, but rather are the unfolding of man's innate potentials. And though humankind's future will bring lessons, some of them hard, we are moving forward into expanding awareness and undreamed of potential.

Over one hundred years ago Yukteswar predicted that we would live in a time of extraordinary change, and that much we believe to be fixed and true — our entire way of looking at the world — would be transformed and uplifted. In *The Yugas*, Selbie and Steinmetz present substantial and intriguing evidence from the findings of historians and scientists that demonstrate the truth of Yukteswar's and Yogananda's revelations.

Millions are wondering what the future holds, and if we are due for a world-changing global shift. Paramhansa Yogananda (author of the classic *Autobiography of a Yogi*) and his teacher, Sri Yukteswar (author of *The Holy Science*), offered key insights into this subject. According to their teachings, we have recently passed through the low ebb in that cycle and are moving to a higher age—an Energy Age that will revolutionize the world.

THE ESSENCE OF SELF-REALIZATION

The Wisdom of Paramhansa Yogananda

Recorded, compiled, and edited by his disciple, Swami Kriyananda

Filled with lessons, stories, and jewels of wisdom that Paramhansa Yogananda shared only with his closest disciples, this volume is an invaluable guide to the spiritual life, carefully organized in twenty main topics.

Great teachers work through their students, and Yogananda was no exception. Swami Kriyananda comments, "After I'd been with him a year and a half, he began urging me to write down the things he was saying during informal conversations." Many of the three hundred sayings presented here are available nowhere else. This book and *Conversations with Yogananda* are must-reads for anyone wishing to know more about Yogananda's teachings and to absorb his wisdom.

REVELATIONS OF CHRIST
Proclaimed by Paramhansa Yogananda
Presented by his disciple, Swami Kriyananda

"The time-tested scriptures of the world are one in essence, inspiring man on his upward journey." — *Autobiography of a Yogi* by Paramhansa Yogananda

Yogananda's mission to the West was to show the oneness of all true religions — especially the unity of the core teachings of original Christianity and original Hinduism. Yogananda's spiritual interpretations of Christ's life and teachings reveal the true meaning of Christ's words, which have been misunderstood for centuries.

There have been two main approaches to studying Jesus' life and teachings: Church authority and historical analysis. But a third, less known method is to study the writings and sayings of saints like Yogananda who have been in direct communion with Christ. *Revelations of Christ* is grounded in this approach.

In this fresh perspective, Swami Kriyananda, direct disciple of Yogananda, explains why the teachings of a religious organization like the Church can be marred by omission, misinterpretation, or a lack of understanding. He then presents Yogananda's "gemstones of Christ's teaching" in all their resplendence.

INTUITION FOR STARTERS
Swami Kriyananda

Every day in our hectic world we are tasked with multiple decisions based on either not enough information or too much information. Problem solving when clear-cut answers are elusive is stressful.

Is there a way to know how to make the best choice? Yes! through developing our faculty of intuition.

Often thought of as something vague and undefinable, intuition is the ability to perceive truth directly not by reason, logic, or analysis, but by simply knowing from within.

This book explains how within each of us lies the ability to perceive the answers we need and shows how to access the powerful stream of creative energy which lies beneath the surface of our conscious mind: the superconscious.

Step-by-step exercises, advice, and guidance reveal the once mysterious faculty of intuition to be an ally and an accessible fountain of wisdom to be found within each of us.

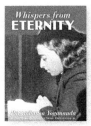

WHISPERS FROM ETERNITY
A Book of Answered Prayers
Paramhansa Yogananda
Edited by his disciple, Swami Kriyananda

Many poetic works can inspire, but few have the power to change lives. These poems and prayers have been "spiritualized" by Paramhansa Yogananda: Each has drawn a response from the Divine. Yogananda was not only a master poet, whose imagery here is as vivid and alive as when first published in 1949: He was a spiritual master, an avatar.

He encouraged his disciples to read from *Whispers from Eternity* every day, explaining that through these verses he could guide them after his passing. But this book is not for his disciples alone. It is for spiritual aspirants of any tradition who wish to drink from this fountain of pure inspiration and wisdom.

THE ESSENCE OF THE BHAGAVAD GITA
Explained by Paramhansa Yogananda
As remembered by his disciple, Swami Kriyananda

Rarely in a lifetime does a new spiritual classic appear that has the power to change people's lives and transform future generations. This is such a book. This revelation of India's best-loved scripture approaches it from a fresh perspective, showing its deep allegorical meaning and down-to-earth practicality. The themes presented are universal: how to achieve victory in life through union with the Divine; how to prepare for life's final exam — death — and what happens afterward; and how to triumph over all pain and suffering.

Swami Kriyananda worked with Paramhansa Yogananda in 1950 while the Master completed his commentary. At that time, Yogananda commissioned him to disseminate his teachings worldwide.

"Millions will find God through this book!" Yogananda declared upon completion of the manuscript. "Not just thousands — millions. I have seen it. I know."

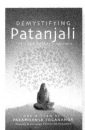

DEMYSTIFYING PATANJALI: THE YOGA SUTRAS
The Wisdom of Paramhansa Yogananda
Presented by his direct disciple, Swami Kriyananda

For millennia this fascinating series of yoga sutras, or aphorisms, by the great Indian sage Patanjali has baffled scholars and mystics alike. Today, these powerful writings stand newly revealed as a practical, concise handbook that redirects all sincere seekers swiftly towards their true home in the Divine.

Demystifying Patanjali represents the confluence of three great yoga teachers. Patanjali, the first exponent of the ancient teachings of yoga, presented his system of inner contemplation, meditation practice, and ethics. Paramhansa Yogananda, perhaps the greatest of all yoga masters to live and teach in the West, revealed with deep insight the meaning behind Patanjali's often obscure aphorisms.

THE ROAD AHEAD

Based on World Prophecies of the Famed Indian Mystic Paramhansa Yogananda
Swami Kriyananda

Whatever the future holds in store for us, one thing is certain: We may look forward to sweeping changes in our lives in the years to come.

Based on the predictions that Paramhansa Yogananda made not to frighten us, but to strengthen us to deal with what lies ahead. Even suffering has its divine purpose: changing harmful habits that keep us imprisoned in lower consciousness. The best preparation of all is to deepen our inner life and attune our individual will with the will of God. Those who do so will come out of this period stronger and freer.

The Road Ahead can be our road map. It shows us how to move forward through the challenges and obstacles in our path toward new horizons of greater spiritual awareness and unity for humanity as a whole.

More Selected Offerings

Touch of Light series
Nayaswami Jyotish and Nayaswami Devi

Affirmations for Self-Healing
Swami Kriyananda

AUM: The Melody of Love
Joseph Bharat Cornell

Change Your Magnetism, Change Your Life
Naidhruva Rush

God Is for Everyone
Inspired by Paramhansa Yogananda
As taught to and understood by his disciple, Swami Kriyananda

How to Meditate
Jyotish Novak

In Divine Friendship
Swami Kriyananda

Lightbearer
Asha Nayaswami

The Need for Spiritual Communities
Swami Kriyananda

The Promise of Immortality
Swami Kriyananda

Religion in the New Age
Swami Kriyananda

The Rubaiyat of Omar Khayyam Explained
Paramhansa Yogananda
Edited by his disciple, Swami Kriyananda

Sharing Nature
Joseph Bharat Cornell

The Yugas
Joseph Selbie and David Steinmetz

Printed in the USA
CPSIA information can be obtained
at www.ICGtesting.com
LVHW020728081023
760313LV00005B/19